Beginner's Gu... Crochet

To Susan, Meryl and Tracey,
my daughters and my friends.

Beginner's Guide to
Crochet
Pauline Turner

SEARCH PRESS

First published in Great Britain 2005

Search Press Limited
Wellwood, North Farm Road,
Tunbridge Wells, Kent TN2 3DR

Text copyright © Pauline Turner 2005
Crochet designs copyright © Pauline Turner 2005

Photographs by Roddy Paine Photographic Studios and
Charlotte de la Bédoyère, Search Press Studios
Photographs and design copyright © Search Press Ltd. 2005

ISBN 1 903975 46 8

The Publishers and author can accept no responsibility for any
consequences arising from the information, advice or instructions
given in this publication.

Readers are permitted to reproduce any of the crochet in this book
for their personal use, or for the purposes of selling for charity, free
of charge and without the prior permission of the Publishers. Any
use of the crochet for commercial purposes is not permitted
without the prior permission of the Publishers.

Suppliers
If you have difficulty in obtaining any of the materials and
equipment mentioned in this book, then please write to the
Publishers, at the address above, for a current list of stockists,
including firms who operate a mail-order service.

Publisher's note
All the step-by-step photographs in this book feature the
author, Pauline Turner, demonstrating crochet. No models
have been used.

Colour separation by Universal Graphics, Singapore
Printed in Malaysia by Times Offset (M) Sdn Bhd

UK edition, using UK terminology

I would like to thank Lynne Tuck for the
design for the pram cover on page 54,
Rita Williams for the design for the child's
top, bag and hair scrunchie on page 50 and
Dr Keith Aubrey for supplying the chart on
page 13 and the symbols used throughout
this book. Thanks also to the staff at
Search Press, Rowan Yarns, Colinette Yarns
and all my students everywhere.

Page 1

Sugar and Spice
*This super top for a favourite little girl is made even more
special by the addition of a matching bag and hair scrunchie.*

Page 3

Super Scarf
*This cuddly scarf made with a large hook and the softest
mohair yarn will be ready to keep away winter chills in no time.*

Page 5

Brilliant Bag
*This versatile bag uses only chain and slip stitch and is really
quick to make.*

Contents

Introduction

In this age of high technology and mechanisation, it is both exciting and a relief to find something that has not followed the trend. Crochet is a wonderful, hands-on experience that uses the sense of touch. A stitch begins and ends with only one loop on the hook, so it can be worked in any direction to create wonderful crunchy textures or fabulous lace. With crochet, you can create all kinds of colour variations using only one yarn at a time. The hook can be inserted anywhere, not just at the top of the stitch. Inserting it over a coloured stripe breaks up the band of colour to produce wonderful designs.

Another twenty-first century trend is the need for everything to be done quickly. Compared to other hand crafts, crochet is fast to work. Early crochet patterns used hooks the same size as knitting needles, but a crochet stitch is half as thick again as a knitted stitch. If you use a larger hook, crochet becomes softer, drapes more easily, uses less yarn and grows rapidly. If you work a crochet stitch incorrectly, but do not spot the mistake until you are halfway through your work, it does not really matter. Carry on using the wrong stitch, and you will still end up with something special. You can worry about using the correct method in future!

As you gain confidence using a hook, the materials you can use will be virtually limitless. When you feel comfortable working crochet, you will be able to use any thickness of yarn, and anything from pure wool, cotton, linen, silk, acrylic and other synthetic fibres to leather, wire, raffia and paper. You should begin with a medium hook and knitting yarn so you can see how the stitches are constructed. The process is the same for the fine threads used in household items as for wide strips of fabric used to produce rugs.

Crochet can be used to customise an 'off the peg' garment, for edgings, braids and buttons, or for decorative motifs on knitted or woven items. It is endlessly versatile, and such an enormous range of articles can be made that crochet should be for everyone.

An example of the versatility of crocheted fabrics.

Materials

Crochet is ideal for anyone who wants a relaxing, enjoyable hobby but does not want to spend a great deal of money. You will need only the minimum of materials to start, and crochet is easily transported so you can do it anywhere.

Hooks

Hooks are now made in international sizes measured in millimetres. There are many sizes and shapes, which can be broken down into three main types:

Regular hooks These come in sizes from 2.00mm to 15.00mm. The body narrows as it merges with the head. They are used mainly for standard yarn but can be used to crochet any continuous strand. Smaller sizes are usually metal and larger sizes plastic. Bamboo or wooden hooks are sometimes available.

Hooks with handles These range in size from 0.60mm to 6.00mm and are ideal for anyone who has difficulty holding a hook for extended periods. As a bonus, the handles are warm to the touch.

Stiletto-shaped hooks (also known as *tambour* or *cotton* hooks) are available in international sizes from 0.60mm to 1.75mm and are used for fine crochet.

Tip
Choosing the right hook needs a little care. The secret is to remember that you are in control, not the hook. Everyone works to a different natural tension, and yours may change when you are more relaxed. If you find your work is tighter than the last time, just use a larger hook until you are able to relax. Next time you may find your work is too loose, so change to a smaller hook!

Hooks
Large plastic hooks, regular hooks, hooks with handles and cotton hooks.

Tip
You may see hooks that are long, like knitting needles. These are used for Tunisian crochet, which is not covered in this book.

Other materials

Crochet requires very little in the way of materials, just a hook, some yarn and a pair of scissors, but you may find it useful to have some of these in your kit.

Tape measure Use this to check the tension of your work. I never use the first few centimetres of a tape measure to measure with as they can easily become frayed or stretched.

Needles A tapestry or sewing needle with a large eye is the best way to fasten in ends. You can also use a small crochet hook to work the yarn ends through to the back of your work.

Pins I use glass-headed pins. They have larger heads than regular dressmakers' pins and this prevents pins from getting 'lost' in longer stitches.

Safety pins I place one of these in the loop of my work to stop it unravelling if I have to leave it.

Buttons The choice of buttons can make a big difference to the look of a finished garment. Plain buttons can be used as a template for your own handmade yarn buttons – see page 59.

Scissors You will need large scissors to cut paper or card for templates and a small, sharp pair to cut off the ends of the yarn. Round-ended scissors are best: otherwise, make sure the points are clear of your work as you snip.

Sequins These can be used to give extra sparkle to many crochet designs – see the Sugar and Spice project on page 50.

Yarns and thread

I advise beginners to choose either double knitting (DK) yarn and a 4.50mm hook, or aran yarn and a 5.50mm hook, in a mixture of wool and acrylic. This will allow the construction of the stitches to be seen easily. Other readily available yarns that are suitable for crochet include 4-ply and No. 10 crochet cotton (sometimes known as bedspread weight).

Choosing yarn

One of the joys of crochet is that you can create beautiful designs using textured yarns that are quite difficult to knit with, such as bouclé. This is very easy to crochet with if you choose a short stitch such as double crochet and a hook large enough to cope with the thickest part of the yarn. Other yarns include 'fashion' ranges, which may be produced for only one season. Fibre content varies, and they may include lots of colours and slubs. They can also be expensive, though you may be able to find discontinued fashion yarn at a reduced price. It is best to avoid these until you can work the basic stitches comfortably and know how to increase and decrease. When you have mastered crochet, fashion yarns can be a source of inspiration.

Yarns are produced in many different fibres. You can also crochet with thread, but this does not stretch so every tension error is visible. Beginners often buy 100% acrylic DK yarn, which is relatively inexpensive and readily available, but has a tendency to stretch. I recommend mixed fibre yarn: it is softer and minor tension differences are not so noticeable, but mistakes are. When you know the basic stitches and feel comfortable working them, there are so many threads and yarns available that there will be no limit to what you can achieve.

Choosing the right hook

For general purposes, try a 5.50mm hook for aran weight yarn, a 4.50mm hook for DK, a 3.50mm hook for 4-ply and a 1.75mm hook for No. 10 cotton. If you want a firmer finish for something like a garment intended to keep out the wind, or a pair of slippers, use a hook up to three sizes smaller. This is a particularly useful tip if you are making household items that will receive hard wear, like rugs or cushion covers. Larger hooks produce softer fabric that drapes easily. This is good for clothing and textiles like curtains, tablecloths and bedspreads that look better when they fall into folds.

Double knitting yarn and a 4.50mm hook are ideal for beginners.

Tip
Hook conversions are not always exact – see the chart on page 13. Believe it or not, some patterns tell you to use hook sizes that are not actually made! The hook size is more important than the yarn, so always check your tension, particularly when you are substituting yarn.

A selection of yarns suitable for crochet

Essentials

Crochet begins with only one loop on the hook. The 'right side' of your work is determined by factors including texture, shaping, or the way the yarn is joined – both sides should look equally neat. If you see the pattern instruction 'RS', mark the right side with thread at once as it may be hard to do this later.

Reading a pattern

Patterns tell you the number and type of stitches and where to put them. All the information you need is given in phrases between commas. Read the pattern carefully before you begin. Some patterns are written in the form of a chart that uses international signs and symbols – see the guide opposite. Work the stitches and place the hook as indicated on the chart. Increases will be shown as two or more stitches in one place. When chains are to be included the chart will give the actual number of chains to work. This may not be the same as the number of chains drawn on the chart.

Beginning a row

Stitches vary in height. The first stitch of a row is represented by a chain or chains: the number may vary according to the type and height of stitches in individual rows.

A stitch is usually worked by inserting the hook under two strands of the 'chain' at the top of the stitch, unless the pattern says otherwise. The fabric will look different according to whether the front or back strands have been picked up, so be consistent. If the pattern says 'in chain space (chsp)', insert the hook in the space *under* the chain, not in the stitch.

Turning chain

Patterns may include a turning chain or chains that count as the first stitch of a row. If the next stitch of the row is worked into the same place as the turning chain it will form an increase. Make turning chains carefully: if the edges of your work are too loose or too tightly gathered it will not hang straight. Only very few pattern designers do not count the turning chain as the first stitch.

Foundation row

In some patterns, you may see the term 'foundation row'. This is worked into the first row of chains, but is usually the same as subsequent rows. If your pattern does not include a foundation row, there is nothing missing – just begin with row 1. Some people like to begin with a row of double crochet, but I prefer to work directly into the starting chain, particularly when using tall stitches. Tall stitches spread, so when they are placed above a row of short stitches, the sides of the fabric tend to splay out. The shorter the stitch, the less play in the fabric.

Pattern repeats

Pattern repeats within rows can be written in different ways. The most usual uses an asterisk, for example: '*2tr, 2ch, miss 2 sts, rep from * to last 2 sts'. This means 'repeat the instructions between the asterisk and comma until you reach the last two stitches'. Another might say something like: '*2tr, 2ch, miss 2 sts, rep from * 4 times'. This means 'work the given stitch pattern, then repeat it four more times'. The other common way to define pattern repeats in a row uses brackets, for example: '(2tr, 2ch, miss 2 sts) 4 times', which means 'work the instructions in the brackets four times'.

Making up

A good crochet pattern needs minimal joining after completion. Yarn produces flexible crocheted fabric, and joining work on the wrong side with double crochet allows the seam to move with the fabric. Avoid joining work using slip stitches or by sewing if possible, as neither is elastic. Lacy fabrics can be joined with chain and double crochet or by sewing. Work made with cotton thread does not have the elasticity of other fibres so can be sewn together.

Crochet can be joined using double crochet worked through two thicknesses.

Crab stitch (see page 75) is an attractive join, especially in a contrasting colour.

12

Common abbreviations

alt alternate

approx approximately

beg beginning

chsp chain space

ch(s) chain(s)

cl cluster

cm centimetres

dc double crochet

dec decrease

DK double knitting

dtr double treble

g gramme/grammes

gr/s group/s

htr half treble

in inch(es)

inc increase

incl including

lp(s) loop(s)

m metre(s)

mm millimetres

p picot

patt pattern

quadtr quadruple treble

rem remains/remaining

rep repeat

rnd round

RS right side (of work)

RtrB raised treble back

RtrF raised treble front

sp space

ss slip stitch

st(s) stitch(es)

tog together

tr treble

trcl treble cluster

trtr triple treble

WS wrong side

yoh yarn over hook

Hook conversions

International (mm)	US size	Old UK size	
		wool	cotton
0.6	14		7
0.75	12		6½
1.00	10		5½
1.25	9		4½
1.5	8	16	3½
1.75	7	15	2½
2.00	4	14	1½
2.50	0	12	0
3.00	B	10	3
3.50	C	9	4
4.00	E	8	5
4.50	F	7	
5.00	G	6	
5.50	-	5	
6.00	H	4	
7.00	I	2	
8.00	K	–	
9.00	L	–	
10.00	N	–	
12.00	P	–	
15.00	Q	–	
17.00	–	–	

Common symbols

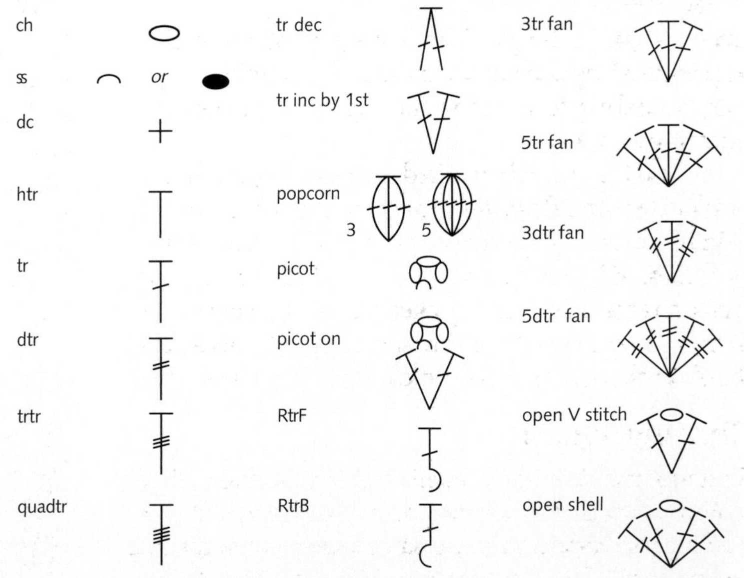

Tip

If the symbols on your pattern are too small to see clearly, use a magnifying glass or enlarge them on a photocopier.

Basic techniques

There are no rules in crochet, only good and bad ways. A good way is one you feel comfortable with, and that produces the effect you want.

HOLDING THE HOOK

There are many ways to hold a hook. How you hold yours is up to you, but these tips may help you to choose. One way is to hold it like a pencil; another is to hold it on top, a bit like a violin bow. If you have not tried crochet before you may feel more comfortable with the first way: as it is like holding a pencil the hook does not feel so strange in the hand.

Tip
If you have not tried crochet before, try my favourite method of holding the hook first. If you are achieving good results with a different method, do not change.

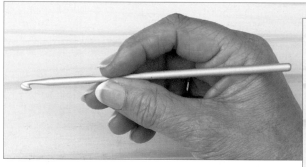

Method 1: holding the hook like a pencil

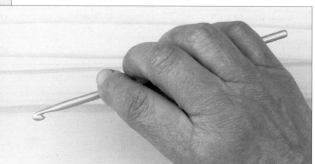

Method 2: holding the hook like a violin bow

THE CORRECT WORKING POSITION

Keep the hook diagonal when you insert it in the stitch, and take care not to lift it before you work off the loops (see example A). If you do not hold the hook on the diagonal (see example B) the loops may become uneven and baggy.

A. Holding the hook correctly

B. Holding the hook incorrectly

HOLDING THE YARN

Cotton yarn has a firm texture with little 'give', but most other yarns have some elasticity which should be incorporated in the stitch. It is important not to hold the yarn too tightly. The most common ways of holding yarn are shown below.

TRADITIONAL METHOD
The work is held by the thumb and index finger or the thumb and middle finger. The yarn is around the little finger. Do not hold the work too tightly or it may create stress in the arm to the shoulder.

MY FAVOURITE METHOD
The work is held by the thumb and index finger. The yarn is taken around two fingers as shown. With this method you do not have to curl the little finger under to stop the yarn falling off the hand.

THE US METHOD
The work is held between the thumb and the middle finger. The yarn is taken around the little finger. The forefinger points upwards, which may mean that some stitches are harder to make.

MEASURING TENSION

Before you make anything, measure your tension. Your pattern will tell you how many stitches you should be producing in a given measurement. Make a test piece large enough to measure accurately: for yarns in weights from 4-ply to aran, I recommend a piece at least 15cm (6in) square. Remember your tension may change after a few rows, particularly when the stitch pattern is new to you.

Lay your work on a smooth, flat surface, not your knee or the arm of a chair, and stroke it gently from the bottom to the top. Do not stroke it widthwise before measuring or the fabric will drop during use and the article will end up too narrow and too long.

Tip
Before measuring, roll the test piece from side to side, then tug gently to elongate the stitches. This produces an effect similar to that of gravity when a finished item is worn.

Measure across the tension square, avoiding the edges as they may be uneven.

Check the tension the other way, taking care not to pull the test piece out of shape.

A small variation in stitch size can make a big difference to a finished piece. Each of these squares was made with the same yarn, but using hooks in different sizes.

SLIP KNOT

All stitches in crochet begin and end with one loop on the hook. Before you start to crochet, you must put a loop on the hook. This is done by making a slip knot, and there are three types:

a) a knot that slips from the short or tail end.
b) a knot that slips from the yarn emerging from the ball.
c) a knot that does not slide at all.

I prefer method a), as it allows the little bump at the beginning of a row to be tightened and hidden. It also means you can make buttons without a central hole.

SLIDING SLIP KNOT

Use this method to make a slip knot with a sliding tail. The completed loop rarely fits snugly on the hook but drawing the short end towards the hook tightens it.

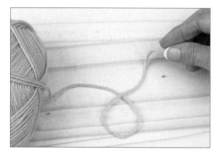

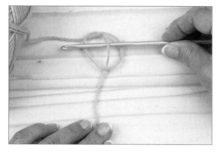

1. Place the loose end of the yarn over the main yarn from the ball to form a loop.

2. Position this end over and behind the loop you have just made.

3. Insert the hook under the single central thread, and over both sides of the loop.

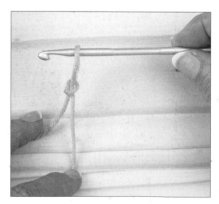

4. Tighten the knot on the hook by holding both the short end of the thread and the thread from the ball, and pulling the hook upwards.

The finished slip knot: note that the short end tightens.

CHAIN STITCH (ch)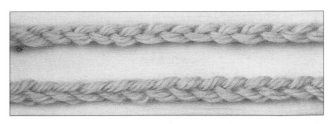

Chains are the foundation for the stitches in most designs, just like casting on in knitting. The stitches of a crochet pattern are worked into the loops of this length of chain. It can also be used to create holes in open and lacy stitch patterns, or for items like fishnet-style tops or bags (see *Brilliant Bags*, page 20). There are three 'families' of stitches in crochet: the first comprises chain stitch (below) and slip stitch (see page 18), and the others are double crochet (see page 24) and treble stitch (see page 32). All crochet stitches are variations of these basic stitches: what changes the look of crochet is where the hook is inserted, how many stitches are missed before another stitch is placed, and the number of stitches worked in one place.

Chain stitches should be the same size as the thickest part of the hook. Try not to make them too tight, or the first row of your work will be narrower than the rest. This could make the hem of a garment like a jacket pull in, giving it a balloon shape that emphasises parts of the body you might prefer to camouflage!

Chain stitch: the top example shows the reverse of a chain; the bottom example is the right side.

USING CHAIN STITCH

One side of the chain looks like an embroidery chain, while the other side is rough. Work with the flat, embroidered-look side of the chain facing, unless the pattern tells you otherwise. Chains are also used at the beginning of a row or round of crochet. In crochet, the hook is at the top of the stitch being made, so at the start of a row or round you need to make chain stitches to lift the hook to the appropriate height. Different crochet stitches vary in height, so the number of chains needed at the start of each row will depend on the stitch chosen.

Tip
One of the best things about crochet is the ease with which you can correct mistakes: you just pull back the faulty stitches and start again.

MAKING A CHAIN (ch)

Begin with a slip knot – see opposite for method.

1. Bring the yarn over the hook from the back to the front.

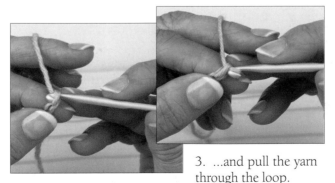

2. Draw the hook smoothly through the loop, gathering the yarn...

3. ...and pull the yarn through the loop.

4. Repeat until you have made as many loops (ch) as you need, not counting the loop on the hook.

SLIP STITCH (ss) ⌒ or ⬤

A slip stitch is the only crochet stitch that does not produce height. It is usually used to connect one stitch to another, or a stitch to another point, and is made by picking up two strands of the stitch it is worked into. This makes the fabric strong, and should be done even when making open fabric. Sometimes you may find a pattern that is entirely in slip stitch. In this case, you should pick up only the back loop of the slip stitch or the fabric will not grow in height.

1. Insert the hook, picking up two strands...

2. ...yoh as for a chain...

3. ...and draw the yarn through all the loops on the hook.

SLIP STITCH CIRCLE

Another use for slip stitch is as a link stitch to join rounds or when you are making tubes – see the chain and slip stitch bag on page 20.

1. Pick up a loop from the end of the chain.

2. Yarn over hook...

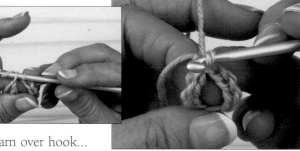

3. ...and pull through to form a circle.

FASTENING OFF

Take care to fasten your work off securely, or all your efforts will be wasted.

1. Cut the yarn leaving a 15cm (6in) length.

2. Work 1 ch...

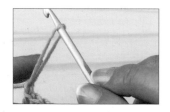

3 ...then pull the end through to form a knot.

4. Slide your finger and thumb down the thread to tighten the knot.

JOINING IN YARN

Tall crochet stitches can use a lot of yarn, so it is wasteful to join in new balls only at the end of rows. For joins in solid fabric, follow the method below. The yarn ends are worked over so you will only be able to recognise the join by feel.

1. Work the stitch until all loops are on the hook.

2. Introduce the new yarn...

3. ...and work off the next two loops.

4. Finish the stitch in the usual way.

5. Remove the hook from the stitch...

6. ...and weave the yarn ends through the back of the work, one by one.

7. Replace the hook and finish the row...

8. ...so the yarn ends are covered by new stitches.

THICK YARN

For thick yarns, weave one end through the back of the work, and one up the side of the last stitch worked and through the tops of the *previous* few stitches. This traps the ends on different rows and gives a neater join.

1. Work the stitch and introduce the new yarn as in the previous example.

2. Weave one yarn end through the back of your work.

3. Turn your work and weave the other end through the previous few stitches.

SEWN JOIN

For lacy patterns, it is best to avoid loose ends. If the yarn is not too thin, sew one end through the other, then pull gently to form a continuous strand.

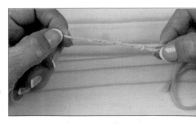

1. Thread one end of the yarn on a needle and...

2. ...weave it in and out of the other yarn end...

3. ...and pull gently to form a continuous strand.

Brilliant Bags

in chain and slip stitch

The quickly made, versatile Coral bag is an attractive accessory that you can simply unfold for use in emergencies. It is made using just slip stitch and chain stitch, worked in a simple tube shape and joined at the lower edge after completion. It can be lined with a toning or contrasting colour.

The White Bag on page 22 has a contrasting lining and tassels to finish it.

Slip stitch is just a variation of a chain, and a lovely open fabric can be made using only chain and slip stitch. The fabric is extremely flexible and does not hold its shape unless it is lined. It is an accommodating fabric that takes the shape of whatever it covers, so it is not recommended for items that need to stay firm. It is, however, the perfect fabric for foldaway shopping bags, loose cover-ups, curtains, garden netting or even string vests!

Coral Bag

Make a slip knot, leaving a 15–20cm (6–8in) yarn end. Work 112ch. Try to ensure that the ch is not twisted.

Row 1: ss into 8th ch from hook, *5ch, miss 3ch, ss in next ch, rep from * to end (27 x 5ch loops).

Row 2 (to form a tube): fold work in half, making sure all the loops face upwards, and that the tighter starting ch is at the bottom. Work 5ch, ss in sp made by the first 8ch lp on row 1. You will now have 28 x 5ch loops. Work *5ch, 1ss in next 5ch sp, rep from * until work measures 40cm (16in). Make sure the final row ends in line with the point where you began (marked by the 15–20cm [6–8in] yarn end).

Finishing row (optional)

Work 5dc into each lp.

Note: this Coral Bag (see the photograph opposite) is finished in this way. The lined White Bag (see page 23) drapes better without a finishing row.

Drawstring handle

Divide the remaining yarn into three small balls. Using a 5.50mm hook and three strands of yarn, make a chain 140cm (55in) long. Fasten off.

To complete

Thread the chain through the loops at the top of the bag. Attach the two ends securely to the bottom. Close the base of the bag by sewing or joining the edges with slip stitch.

You will need

150g DK weight cotton yarn

4.50mm hook

Size: width 33cm (13in) length 40cm (16in)

Tension: 2 x 5chsp lps measure 5cm (2in); 4 rows (2 diamonds) measure 3.5cm (1½ in)

Note: the tension given is approximate because of the fabric's flexibility.

Cast-on chain and foundation row

Second row added

Coral Bag
This quickly made, unlined bag folds out for use in seconds.

White Bag

Leaving a 15–20cm (6–8in) yarn end, work 88ch.
Row 1: work as for the Coral Bag until there are 21 x 5ch loops.
Row 2: form a tube as for row 2 of the Coral Bag (22 x 5ch lps) *5ch, 1ss in next 5chsp, rep from * until work measures 30cm (12in).

Handle and drawstring

With the 5.50mm hook and four strands of yarn, work a 50cm (19½ in) ch. Make another ch 1m (39in) long using two strands of yarn.

Tassels

Make two small tassels. For each one, wrap yarn eighteen times around a piece of card 5cm (2in) deep. Slide the yarn loops off and secure about a third of the way down the tassel using a separate piece of yarn. Cut the loops that are away from the short end. Make two larger tassels in the same way but using a 10cm (4in) piece of card.

To complete

Using the lining fabric, make a bag to fit inside the crochet. Attach to the inside top of the bag, leaving 2–3 rows free as a decorative border. Attach a large tassel to each corner of the base, catching the corner of the lining at the same time. Secure the handle on either side of the bag. Thread the drawstring through your work, three rows down and starting at the centre point of one side. This will be the front of the bag. Add a small tassel to each end of the drawstring.

You will need

150g DK weight cotton yarn

4.50mm and 5.50mm hooks

Piece of card 10cm (4in) deep

Piece of card 5cm (2in) deep

Cotton fabric: 0.5m (18in) for lining

Size: width 23cm (9in); length 30cm (12in)

Tension: 2 x 5chsp loops measure 5cm (2in); 4 rows (2 diamonds) measure 3.5cm (1½ in)

MAKING TASSELS

1. Wind the yarn around a cardboard template.

2. Thread a needle on one yarn end. Remove the yarn from the template.

3. Wrap the yarn end around the bundled yarn.

4. Sew the threaded yarn through to secure the end.

5. Cut through the tassel end with scissors.

The finished tassel

The finished White Bag

This bag has been lined with a contrasting material which gives it a firmer finish.

DOUBLE CROCHET (dc) +

This is the second of the crochet stitch 'families'. When you have learned to work dc, you will be able to make the colourful tablemats (see page 28 for instructions).

To begin, make a chain for every stitch you need, plus one. With the smooth side of the chain facing, insert the hook in the *third* chain along. The 'missed' chain will count as the first stitch of the row (one base chain plus one chain to give the height of the dc). Always count the turning chain or chains as the first stitch of a row, unless your pattern says otherwise.

1. Make a length of chain.

2. Insert the hook, front to back, in the third chain from the hook...

3. ...picking up two strands of yarn. Yoh...

4. ...and pull the yarn through...

5. ...to the front.

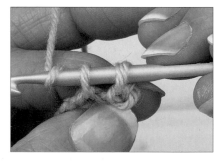

6. Yoh...

Tip
When I have to leave work, I place a safety pin in the last loop to secure it.

7. ...and pull through to finish the stitch. Continue to work 1dc in each chain until you have used all the chains.

Turning your work

After the first row of dc, your work will look like a neat cord. Adding more rows will produce fabric. Follow the steps below to turn your crochet and work the second row, remembering that the first dc is worked in the *second* stitch of the row. Repeat this row to the required length.

1. Make 1ch, which will serve as the first stitch of the next row.

2. Turn your work *under*, keeping the hook steady and the loop on the hook.

3. Insert the hook in the next stitch.

4. Yoh, then pull through to finish (see step 7 opposite).

Finding the last stitch in a row

To keep the sides of your work straight, you must be able to recognise the last stitch of a row. The best way to do this is to make the turning chain or chains *before* you turn your work to go back. Though turning chains count as the first stitch of a row, making them at the end of the row *before* means that the smooth side will be facing when you work the last stitch of the next row.

1. Work a stitch in the last *hole* of the row, but do not stop – you still have another stitch to go!

2. To work the last stitch, insert the hook under the top two loops of the turning chain. Work the stitch, and then turn.

Counting rows and stitches

When you look at a piece of double crochet, you will see strong, straight lines at regular intervals. Each of these lines equals two rows. Between the unbroken lines you will see a line of dashes: each dash is a stitch. Count the turning chain as a stitch, and remember to include the very last 'dash'.

Double crochet fabric: each 'line' you can see equals two rows; each 'dash' is a stitch.

CRAB STITCH

This stitch gives a wonderful finish when it is used as an edging or finishing row – see the yellow tablemat on page 29. It produces a whipped effect that is more pronounced when the right side is facing. Crab stitch is really just double crochet worked backwards, that is from left to right instead of right to left. It may also be known as reverse double crochet, corded edge, rope stitch, Russian or shrimp stitch.

Use a hook one size smaller than for your main fabric. If you are using crab stitch on a single edge, work one turning chain at the end of the previous row. Crab stitch worked in the round can be joined using a slip stitch. There is no need to make an extra chain at the corner when working a square or rectangle as the stitch is very flexible.

Crab stitch edging on double crochet

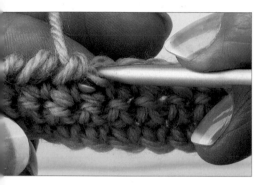

1. Take the hook to the next stitch on the right and insert under two strands of the yarn, ensuring the loop does not fall off.

2. Holding the yarn taut with your forefinger, drop the head of the hook on to the yarn...

3. ...and bring it through to the front (two loops on the hook). You will need to angle the hook as shown.

4. Bring the hook back up to a normal working position.

5. Yoh and draw through the two loops...

6. ...to complete the stitch.

Tip
When working the stitch, take care not to pull the yarn through all the loops at once as this will turn it into a backward slip stitch.

DOUBLE CROCHET RIB

Double crochet fabric is flat and has no elasticity, but if you put your hook into a different place in the stitch it produces a ridged effect. Fabric worked like this becomes elasticated and can be used for welts and cuffs. These are worked as narrow strips in a different direction from the rest of the fabric. To increase the elasticity of rib, use a smaller hook. Work the first row into a starting chain exactly as for dc (see page 24). Work one chain, then turn.

1. Insert the hook under the back loop only of the next stitch.

2. Yoh and pull through (two loops on the hook).

3. Complete as for steps 6–7, page 24. Repeat to the end, work 1ch.

TURNING DOUBLE CROCHET RIB

There are exceptions to many rules, and when it comes to turning, this pattern is one of them. It is important to go into the right place at the beginning of the row, and to find the right stitch at the end of the row. The photographs below should help you to avoid problems.

1. Turn the work *towards* you and insert the hook into the third stitch along, counting the turning chain as the first stitch.

2. Yoh as above, then work the stitch in the normal way. Work 1dc in the back loop of each stitch to the end of the row.

3. Work the last stitch into the back of the 'knot' made by the turning chain.

Terrific Tablemats

in double crochet

All three of these colourful mats use double crochet to create very different looks. The first mat is worked in standard double crochet fabric in yellow, with a green border worked in double crochet completed with a final row of crab stitch. The second mat is worked in double crochet rib using variegated yarn. The third mat is worked in stripes in six different colours, changing the colour on each row. The length of yarn left at the beginning and end of each row is incorporated in the fringe later. When you work with colours in this way, each side of the work looks different so it is reversible.

Tip

Wool or cotton yarn may be substituted for acrylic yarn, but you may need a larger quantity as acrylic fibres tend to weigh less.

Mat 1: with a contrasting border

Make 47ch using M.
Row 1: 1dc in 3rd ch from hook, 1dc in each ch to end (46 sts), 1ch, turn.
Row 2: 1dc in each st to end, 1ch, turn.
Rep row 2 until work measures 20cm (8in). Fasten off.

Border

Rnd 1: Join contrast to corner of foundation ch. Work 1dc in each ch to the corner picking up the remaining strand of each ch, 1dc in same place as last st, dc up the side of mat, spacing it so there are 3dc across every 4 row ends, 1dc in same place as last dc at corner, 1dc in each st to corner, 1dc in same place as last st, dc down the side of the mat working 3dc across 4 row ends. Join with ss, 1ch, turn.
Rnd 2: *1dc in each st to corner, 3dc in corner st, rep from * to end working 2dc only in last st (the 1ch counts as the first dc).
Rnd 3: Do not turn work. Crab st around edge (see page 26). Fasten off.

Note: this crab stitch border is worked using the same size hook as the mat. This allows plenty of ease, so it is not necessary to work an extra stitch at the corners.

You will need

Mat 1

75g aran weight acrylic yarn in main colour (M)

25g of the same yarn in a contrasting colour (C)

4.50mm crochet hook

Size: 35cm x 25cm (14 x 10in)

Tension: 7 sts and 8 rows measure 5cm (2in) worked over dc on 4.50mm hook

Instructions for Mat 2 and Mat 3 begin on page 30.

The finished tablemats

This selection of brightly coloured mats would brighten up any table. From left to right are: Mat 1 in yellow with a green border; Mat 2 in blue and green space-dyed yarn and Mat 3 with its stripes and fringe.

Mat 2: in space-dyed yarn

Make 51ch.
Row 1: 1dc in 3rd ch from hook, 1dc in each ch to end (50sts), 1ch, turn.
Row 2: *1dc in back lp of next st, rep from * to end, 1ch, turn.
Rep row 2 until work measures 25cm (10in). Fasten off.

You will need

Mat 2

100g aran weight space-dyed acrylic yarn

4.50mm hook

Size: 35 x 25cm (14 x 10in)

Tension: 7 sts and 9 rows measure 5cm (2in)

Mat 3: striped with a fringe

Make 51ch
Row 1: 1dc in 3rd ch from hook, 1dc in each ch to end (50sts). Fasten off, leaving a long end (to be incorporated in the fringe).

Row 2: join in another colour leaving a long end for the fringe, 1ch, 1dc in each st to end. Fasten off, leaving a long end for the fringe.
Rep row 2 until work measures 25cm (10in), changing yarn colour on every row and leaving a long end to make a fringe at each side of the mat.

To complete

Add the fringe following the steps opposite, alternating colours to match the stripes on the mat. Incorporate lengths of yarn left at the end of each row by pulling them as you make each 'tassel' of fringe. This saves time sewing in lots of yarn ends! Trim the fringe neatly.

You will need

Mat 3

Oddments of DK-weight yarn in several complementary colours

4.50mm hook

Size: 35 x 25cm (14 x 10in)

Tension: 7 sts and 8 rows to 5cm (2in)

Tip
To make a fuller fringe, hook a doubled-over piece of yarn of the same colour into each side of the row, on every row.

Detail of the worked fringe

ADDING SIMPLE STRIPES

When you work stripes it is not necessary to cut the yarn on each row unless each stripe is a single row of colour – see Mat 3. If you leave long ends of yarn at the beginning and end of each row, they can be incorporated in the fringe.

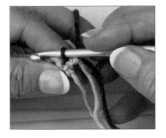

1. Insert the hook and draw the new colour through.

2. Work 1 dc in each stitch to the end.

3. Fasten off the work at the end of the row leaving a length of yarn.

4. Turn the work on each row and introduce the new colour as in step 1.

5. Work the sequence of stripes, linking the fringe on every alternate stitch.

MAKING A BASIC FRINGE

Decide how long you want your fringe to be, then cut a cardboard template – see Making tassels on page 22 – and wrap the yarn around. Cut the lengths of yarn and use a crochet hook to pull them through your work to make the fringe.

1. Fold three cut lengths of yarn in half. Insert the hook...

2. ...and use it to pull the folded yarn through.

3. Tighten the loop by pulling gently...

4. ...to finish each segment of fringe.

TREBLE STITCH (tr) 3 TURNING CH

The last stitch 'family' is the treble, which includes the long trebles and the half treble. Many traditional cotton patterns use taller stitches to create lace. Another use for the taller stitches is to create texture.

Wrapping the yarn around the hook before inserting it makes the stitch taller. The more times you do this, the taller the stitch. The first stitch of a row is represented by a chain or chains that equal the height of the pattern stitch. The taller the stitch, the more of these 'turning' chains you will need: a treble usually needs three, a double treble four and a triple treble five.

WORKING TREBLE

Make a foundation row of chains equal to the number of stitches plus three chains: one to represent the first stitch and two more to equal the height of a treble. A common mistake in the second row of treble is to put the first stitch in the same place as the turning chain. If you do this, the number of stitches will increase with every row and the edge will not be straight: the first treble must be placed in the stitch next to the turning chain. Work 1tr in each stitch to the end of the row, then 3ch before you turn. The last stitch of the second and subsequent rows must be placed in the top of the turning chain from the last row.

Tip
You may not always need three turning chains: if, after a few rows, you notice that there is a 'hole' at the start of each row, try turning with 2ch instead.

The foundation row of chains

1. Yoh, insert the hook in the *fourth* chain from the hook.

2. Yoh as shown above...

3. ...and pull through (three loops on the hook).

4. Yoh and pull through two loops (two loops left on the hook as shown).

5. Yoh and pull through the last two loops to complete the stitch.

TURNING AND WORKING THE SECOND ROW OF TREBLE

1. Turn your work *away* from you.

2. Insert the hook in the stitch *next* to the turning chain. Yoh, pull through two loops...

3. ...yoh to finish the stitch...

4. ...then place the last stitch in the top of the turning chain.

HALF TREBLE (htr) ⊤

2 TURNING CH

This stitch is halfway between a double crochet and a treble. It makes a firm fabric with many different uses. Half treble looks different from other stitches because the top chain of a completed row has three strands rather than two. To give your stitches a firm base, pick up two of these three strands. It does not matter which two strands you choose, but take care to insert the hook in the same way for each stitch.

1. Yoh and insert in the third chain along.

2. Yoh again...

3. ...and pull it through to the front (three loops on the hook).

4. Yoh as for treble, but pull through *all three loops at once*.

5. Work to the end of the row.

DOUBLE TREBLE (dtr) 4 TURNING CH

The next stitch in order of height is the double treble. It is worked in the same way as the treble, but the yarn is wrapped around the hook twice before it is inserted to work the first stitch. Work the first double treble of the first row into the fifth chain from the hook. At the end of the row, turn with four chain.

1. Wrap the yarn around the hook twice...

2. ...and insert the hook in the fifth chain along.

3. Yoh...

4. ...and pull it through to the front (four loops on the hook).

5. Yoh...

6. ...and pull through two loops (three loops on the hook), yoh again as shown.

7. Yoh, pull through two loops (two loops on the hook), yoh again...

8. ...and pull through the last two loops to complete the stitch.

The completed double trebles

TRIPLE TREBLE (trtr) 5 TURNING CH

Again, stitch height is decided by the number of times the yarn is placed over the hook. Work the first stitch in the *sixth* chain from the hook, and turn with 5ch.

1. Yoh *three* times. Insert the hook in the *sixth* chain from the hook.

2. Yoh, pull through to the front (five loops on the hook).

3. Yoh, pull through two loops (four loops on the hook).

4. Yoh, pull through two loops (three loops on the hook).

5. Yoh, pull through two loops (two loops on the hook).

6. Yoh and complete the stitch as shown.

The finished triple trebles

QUADRUPLE TREBLE (quadtr) 6 TURNING CH

This very tall stitch is produced by wrapping the yarn over the hook four times. The first loop tends to stretch as you work off the other loops – to prevent this, keep your finger on the yarn as you wrap it around so each wrap stays the same size as the hook stem. Take your finger off the wraps only as you work them.

1. Yoh *four* times. Insert the hook in the *seventh* chain from the hook.

2. Yoh, pull through to front (six loops on hook). Yoh, pull through two loops. Repeat five times.

The finished quadruple trebles

Note: Treble stitches can be made as tall as you like. For a quintuple treble, wrap the yarn around the hook five times before you insert it. For a sextuple treble, wrap the yarn around the hook six times and so on. Work off the stitches as for treble, pulling through two loops at a time.

Super Scarves

These gorgeous scarves are amazingly quick to make using thick yarn and large hooks. The mohair used for the large scarf in shades of purple lends itself to longer, looser stitches. Mohair should normally be worked using a large hook so the hair in the fibre can breathe and is not trapped and flattened. The shorter neckwarmer in variegated yarn is ideal to carry as a 'just in case' against cool breezes as it takes up very little room. It is folded lengthwise after completion and sewn down one edge to create a double thickness that is really cosy.

Large Scarf

Work 52ch.

Row 1: 1dtr 1ch 1dtr in 5th ch from hook, * miss 2ch, 1dtr 1ch 1dtr in next ch, rep from * to last 2 sts, 1dtr in last st, 4ch, turn.

Row 2: *1dtr 1ch 1dtr in 1ch sp, rep from * to last st, 1dtr in last st.
Rep row 2 until scarf is length required.

Fringe

Cut 50cm (19½ in) lengths of yarn and use the hook to pull three doubled-over strands though each large hole, plus each of the two end holes.

The finished Large Scarf is perfect to liven up a plain winter coat, and also makes a stunning evening wrap with a little black dress.

You will need

Large scarf

200g Colinette mohair

7.00mm hook

Size: 52cm x 130cm (20½ x 52in) without fringe

Tension: 7grs and 7 rows measure 20cm (8in)

Neckwarmer

Work 31ch.
Work rows 1 and 2 of the scarf pattern until the neckwarmer measures 70cm (28in). Fasten off.

To complete
Fold the crochet lengthwise and sew the top, sides and bottom together.

You will need

Neckwarmer

150g Colinette Pure Wool Slub Chunky

7.00mm hook

Size: 13cm x 70cm (5 x 28in), folded in half lengthwise

Tension: 7grs and 7 rows measure 20cm (8in)

The finished Neckwarmer

INCREASES AND DECREASES

One way to shape crochet is by using increases or decreases. These should be worked at the beginning *and* end of the relevant row to produce smooth diagonal or curved edges. If you do not shape crochet evenly, it will be very noticeable as the stitches have different heights.

For simple increases, follow these steps.

1. Insert the hook in the tiny hole between the turning chain and the first stitch.

2. Work the stitch into this hole to produce a neat increase as shown.

3. Work to the end of the row. Place the last stitch in the top of the turning chain of the previous row.

4. Work a second stitch in the same place to produce a neat increase.

USING TURNING CHAINS

To increase by more than one stitch at each side of your work, add one chain for each extra stitch to the turning chain at the beginning of the row. Then use a spare piece of yarn to make a length of chain and attach to the other side. Work into the first extension, over the body of your crochet, and over the extension made with the spare yarn. This type of increase is used for the coat on page 60.

Tip
Increases in lacy or complex patterns will be written out fully in the pattern.

1. Work as many extra chains as you require, then work the turning chain.

2. Turn and work the additional stitches into the extra chains...

3. ...then work into the first stitch of the main part of the crochet.

4. Continue across...

  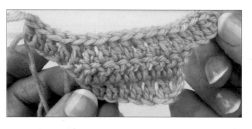

5. ...and into the last stitch of the main part.

6. Work across the chain extension...

7. ...to produce a neat, even increase and ensure that both sides of your work match.

TREBLE DECREASES

Older crochet patterns may tell you to decrease by slip stitching over a certain number of stitches at the beginning of a row and stopping before the end. This produces a step rather than a curve. A better way to decrease, that does not leave holes or create steps, is to draw two or more stitches together at the top. To decrease over two trebles, work the first treble until there are two loops on the hook, work the next to the same stage, then draw the yarn through all three loops on the hook. To decrease three trebles together, work a cluster – see page 48 – over three consecutive trebles, pulling all three together at the top.

The finished decrease

1. Work the first decrease stitch until there are two loops left on the hook.

2. Work the second stitch to the same stage (three loops left on the hook).

3. Yoh...

4. ...and draw through all three loops.

HALF TREBLE DECREASES

The half treble is made by drawing the yarn through three loops all at once rather than two at a time, so it is decreased in a slightly different way. At the start of a row, work an 'unfinished' dc, then an 'unfinished' htr, and pull them together. At the end, work an 'unfinished' htr, then an 'unfinished' dc, and pull together.

The top of a row of half treble

1. Work an 'unfinished' double crochet...

2. ...then an 'unfinished' half treble.

3. Yoh and draw through four loops...

4. ...to produce a neat decrease at the start.

5. Work the next to last stitch as an 'unfinished' half treble.

6. Work the last stitch as an 'unfinished' double crochet.

7. Yoh and pull through all four loops on hook...

8. ...to produce a neat decrease at the end.

ADDING COLOUR

Using colour gives you freedom of choice, and this is particularly true of crochet. No matter how many colours you want to introduce, there is no need to work with more than one at a time, or to carry yarn along the back of rows. Simple striped fabric can be made by changing colour every second row, carrying the yarn not in use up the side of the work and picking it up next time you need it. Do not pull this yarn too tightly or it may pucker.

Crochet fabric should look neat on both sides. If you work a border or join the edges of fabric, this covers the yarn ends so you do not even need to sew them in.

Tip
Stripes can be given a different look if you use stitches of different heights – see Connecting ovals and Catherine wheels on page 42 – or increase and decrease in the same row.

JOINING IN A NEW COLOUR

When you want to change colour, add the new colour *before* you complete the last stitch of the previous row. This is because of the turning chains that represent the first stitch of each row. If you add a new colour *after* completing the last stitch of the previous row, part of the chain will be the old colour and part the new. This will make the previous colour 'bleed' into the row you are working.

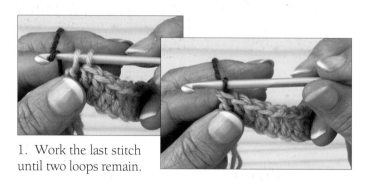

1. Work the last stitch until two loops remain.

2. Introduce the new colour by pulling through both loops.

JOINING IN YARN IN THE MIDDLE OF A ROW

The method above can also be used to join in yarn in the middle of a row. Work to the stitch before you want to introduce the new colour.

1. Work the stitch until there are two loops left. Introduce the new yarn to work off the stitch.

2. Begin to work the next stitch in the new yarn...

3. ...and complete it as shown.

CHANGING COLOUR

When you make striped or patterned fabric by changing colour on every row, there is no need to cut off the yarn. Carry it up the side of your work and join it in as necessary: the result will be far neater and easier than trying to deal with lots of yarn ends. Practise this by working a simple striped fabric, the two-colour trial piece below or one of the examples on page 42.

one of the examples on page 42.

Tip
When working striped or patterned fabric, it is not always necessary to turn your work on every row.

TRIAL PIECE

Row 1: using M, make 17ch. 1tr in 4th ch from hook, tr to end (15 sts). Join in C before you complete the last st (see opposite). Turn, without making any turning ch.
Row 2: *1tr, 1ss, rep from * to end, place the last loop on a safety pin. Do not turn.
Row 3: insert hook in first st. Using M, work 3ch. Work 1tr in each st, yoh, insert hook in last tr. *Before* you bring yarn to front, place lp from safety pin on hook, yoh, draw yarn through this lp and st from row below to lock it, yoh and pull through 2 lps (2 lps rem on hook). Bring up C to complete st, 1ch, turn.
Note: Check the stitch count before you work the last st of the row.
Row 4: dc to end, leave loop in a safety pin.
Row 5: as row 3.
Row 6: as row 2.
Rows 3–6 form patt.

Texture is created by using taller treble stitches between slip stitches, which have no height. Push the treble to the back of the work as it is made to give a more pronounced 'bump'.

Working the piece

1. Do not turn the work at the end of row 2. For row 3, insert the hook in the first stitch (turning chain).

2. Work 3ch, insert the hook to the *right* of the next stitch.

3. Tr to the end. Insert the hook in the last stitch, remove the loop from the safety pin. Place on hook.

4. Yoh and pull through the loop from the safety pin *and* the stitch from the row below.

5. Work the stitch until two loops remain, then bring up the new colour.

6. Pull it through ready to work the chain that will represent the first stitch.

Tip
It is characteristic of crochet that stitches are not made directly on top of each other. When you are turning your work on each row, the stitches are made slightly to the left of the main stem of the stitch. If you are not turning your work, the hook should be inserted slightly to the right of the main stem.

CONNECTING OVALS

Make 21ch in colour 1 (a multiple of 8 sts plus 5).
Row 1: 1dc in 3rd ch from hook, 2dc, *4tr, 4dc, rep from * once, 1ch, turn.
Row 2: 3dc, *4tr, 4dc, rep from * once, change to colour 2, 3ch, turn.
Row 3: 3tr, *4dc, 4tr, rep from * once, 3ch, turn
Row 4: 3tr, *4dc, 4tr, rep from * once, change to colour 1, 1ch, turn.
Row 5: 3dc, *4tr, 4dc, rep from * once, 1ch, turn.

Note: rows 2–5 inclusive form the pattern. If you want to make a larger item, add 8 ch for every stitch pattern repeat.

CATHERINE WHEELS

Make 27ch (a multiple of 10 sts plus 7) in colour 1.
Row 1: 1dc in 2nd ch from hook, 1dc in next ch, *miss 3ch, 7tr in next ch, miss 3ch, 3dc, rep from * to last 4ch, miss 3ch, 4tr in last ch, change to colour 2, turn.
Row 2: 1ch, 1dc, *3ch, work 1cl over the next 7 sts (see page 48), 3ch, 3dc, rep from * to last 4 sts, 3ch, 1cl over 4 sts, turn.
Row 3: 3ch, 3tr in same place, *miss 3ch, 3dc, miss 3ch, 7tr in loop of cl, rep from * to last 5 sts, miss 3ch, 2dc, change to colour 1, turn.
Row 4: 3ch, 1cl over 3 sts, *3ch, 3dc, 3ch. 1cl over 7 sts, rep from * to last 2 sts, 3ch, 2dc, turn.
Row 5: 1ch, 1dc, * miss 3ch, 7tr in loop of cl, miss 3ch, 3dc, rep from * to last st, 4tr in last st. Change to colour 2, rep rows 2–5 incl to length required.

CHEVRONS

Make 24ch in colour 1 (a multiple of 10 sts plus 4).
Row 1: 1tr in 4th ch from hook, *3tr, tr3tog, 3tr, 3tr in next ch, rep from * to end finishing with 2tr in last st, 3ch, turn.
Row 2: 1tr in same place as turning ch, *3tr, tr3tog, 3tr, 3tr in next st, rep from * to end, finish with 2tr in last st, 3ch, turn.

Tip
Start this pattern immediately from the foundation chain. Increasing and decreasing by the same number of stitches on each repeat 'bends' the work. Centre the top point (3tr gr) and bottom point (tr3tog) of each chevron in the chevron on the previous row.

Spike stitch

Using spike stitch can change stripes into geometric designs. It is usually worked over rows of double crochet and, depending on how you place the hook, you can create squares, rectangles, triangles and diamonds. Try working the first row of the border of the tablemat on page 28 in spike stitch, or use it to make attractive button and buttonhole bands on a cardigan or jacket.

Working the spikes

Follow the steps below to work the stitch used for the Snug Rug on page 44.

1. On row 5, work the longest spike just above the foundation chain.

2. For the next spike, insert the hook in the stitch three rows below the top of the work.

3. Pull the yarn to the front. Lift the hook to the top of the work so the yarn is neat and loose.

4. For the next stitch, insert the hook two rows below the top of the work.

5. For the shortest spike stitch, insert the hook one row below the top.

6. Work the last stitch as a normal dc.

Castle spike stitch

Try this variation for the rug overleaf.

Using main colour yarn (M), make 25ch (24 sts).
Row 1: 1dc in 3rd ch from hook, dc to end, 1ch, turn.
Rows 2–4: work in dc, changing to contrast colour (C) on last stitch of last row.
†Row 5: 1ch to act as first dc, 3dc, *4dc into base of sts of row 1, 4dc, rep from * once, 4dc into base of sts of row 1, 1ch, turn.
Rows 6–8: work 3 rows dc, change to M.
Row 9: work 3dc into top of sts in row 4 to cover strip worked in C completely, *4dc, work 4dc into top of sts of row 4, rep from * once, 4dc, 1ch, turn.
Work 3 rows dc, changing to C on last st of last row ††.
Rep from † to †† until the work is the required length.

Snug Rugs

This rug is suitable for any room in the house: try different pastel colour combinations for a nursery, restful neutrals for a study or bright primary colours for a small child's room. It uses spike stitch – see page 43 – to produce an interlocking diamond effect (diamond spike stitch). I worked the rug shown in soft double knitting yarn, but for a different effect it can be worked in any yarn of double knitting weight – see the variation in cotton on page 46 which makes an ideal bath mat.

Fringed Rug

With M and the 4.50mm hook, make 130ch

Row 1: 1dc in 3rd ch from hook, 1dc in each ch to end, 1ch, turn.

Row 2: dc to end, joining in C in last st, 1ch, turn.

Work 4 rows dc, changing back to M in the last st of the 4th row, 1ch, turn.

Row 7 (spike stitch): *1dc in row below, 1dc 2 rows below, 1dc 3 rows below (top of previous colour band), 1dc 2 rows below, 1dc in row below, 1dc, rep from * 12 times, 1ch, turn.

Work 3 rows dc, looping yarn neatly up side of work. Change back to C in the last st of the 3rd row.

Row 11 (spike stitch): *1dc 3 rows below (top of previous colour band), 1dc 2 rows below, 1dc in row below, 1dc, 1dc in row below, 1dc 2 rows below, rep from * 12 times, 1ch, turn.

Work 3 rows dc, looping yarn neatly up the side of work. Change back to M in the last st of the 3rd row.

Rows 4 to 11 form the pattern. Rep them until work measures 90cm (36in).

Border

Using M and with RS facing, work dc up each side of the rug, spacing it so there are 3dc across every 4 row ends. Crab stitch back. Fasten off.

Fringe

Using equal quantities of M and C, cut lengths of yarn to fringe the top and bottom of the rug. I cut 50cm (17in) lengths but this can vary according to preference. Take one strand each of M and C and double over. Hook the loop end through a stitch, then pull the cut strands through the loop. Pull gently to tighten. Repeat, spacing fringing evenly along the edge of the mat.

Top and base edge

Rnd 1: join yarn to a corner and work 2dc in same place. Continue up side in dc, spacing it so there are 3dc across every 4 row ends. Join with ss.

Rnd 2: crab stitch around the edge – no extra corner sts required. Fasten off.

You will need

500g soft DK yarn in main colour (M)

500g soft DK yarn in contrasting colour (C)

4.50mm hook

Size: 50 x 92cm (19½ x 32in)

Tension: 8 sts and 7 rows measure 5cm (2in) worked over dc on 4.50mm hook

Tip
If you do not want to finish your rug with a border, fasten off the yarn for each band of colour.

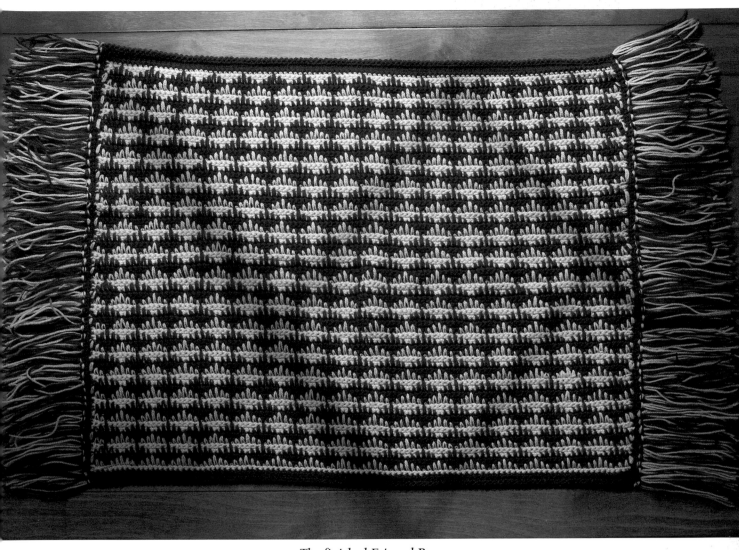

The finished Fringed Rug

The spike stitch used in this pattern creates an illusion of diamonds. A pattern will only appear as diamonds if at least one of the spike stitches in a group covers the whole of the band of colour in the stripe below.

Bathroom Rug

This rug is made from soft cotton which feels luxurious under bare feet and soaks up any little spills. The spike stitches are placed to give the illusion of diagonal triangles (triangle spike stitch). As this pattern uses three colours you may prefer to cut off the ends – trying to carry them up the side of your work could lead to tangles.

Rug

Using A, make 73 ch.
Row 1: 1dc in 3rd ch from hook, 1dc in each ch to end, 1ch, turn (72 sts).
Row 2: 1 dc in each st to end, 1ch, turn.
Rep row 2 twice, joining in B before end of last st.
Row 5 (spike stitch): *1dc 2 rows below, 1dc 3 rows below, 1dc 4 rows below (i.e. in the base of the st in the foundation ch), rep from * to end, 1ch, turn.
Work 3 rows dc, joining in C in last dc of 3rd row, 1ch, turn.
Row 9 (spike stitch): *1dc 4 rows below (top of previous colour band), 1dc 3 rows below, 1dc 2 rows below, rep from * to end, 1ch turn.
Work 3 rows dc joining in A in last dc of 3rd row, 1ch, turn.
Row 13 (spike stitch): *1dc 2 rows below, 1dc 3 rows below, 1dc 4 rows below (top of previous colour band), rep from * to end, 1ch, turn.
Rep rows 6–13 inclusive, changing colours in the sequence ABC at the same time. End the rug design with row 13.
Using A, work 1 row of dc.
Rows 4 to 11 form patt. Rep these 8 rows until work measures as close to 92cm (32in) as possible, ending with row 11.
Note: rows 6–13 form patt, but the colour change covers 12 rows.

Border

Rnd 1: using A and with RS facing, work 1dc in each st across top and bottom edge of rug, 2dc in each corner st, 1 dc in each st up side of rug, spacing dc so there are 3dc over every 4 row ends. Join with ss.
Next rnd: crab stitch around edge – no extra sts needed at corners.
Fasten off.

To complete

If you cut off the yarn ends, sew these in before working the border. An alternative is to loop ends through with a small crochet hook, then work the border over them. The dc will enclose the ends and give a neat finish.

You will need

200g soft cotton DK yarn in colour A

200g soft cotton DK yarn in colour B

200g soft cotton DK yarn in colour C

4.50mm hook

Size: 50 x 92cm (19½ x 32in)

Tension: 8 sts and 7 rows measure 5cm (2in) worked over dc on 4.50mm hook

Tip
If you do not want a finishing border for your mat, fasten off the yarn as you complete each band of colour.

Opposite
The finished Bathroom Rug.

CLUSTERS

Clusters are used to add texture to a variety of crochet fabrics. They are formed when stitches are drawn together at the top, and may be grouped in a single base stitch – the most usual way – or spread over a number of stitches. The number in front of the abbreviation shows how many stitches to use. The three treble cluster (3trcl) is the most popular, though four, five or more stitches can be used. Clusters worked into one stitch are best made with the wrong side of the work facing. They can also be used for decreasing – see page 39.

A standard 3trcl needs a turning chain the same height as the stitches between the clusters. A 3trcl in a row of dc needs only one turning chain, but a 3trcl in a row of trebles needs three turning chains.

see page 39

Tip
Clusters are more pronounced when they are set in rows of shorter stitches. For a cluster that stands out effectively in treble fabric, try making it with four *double* trebles.

1. Insert the hook in the stitch, yoh...

2. ...and pull through to the front (three loops on the hook).

3. Yoh and pull through two loops...

4. ...yoh and insert the hook in the same stitch.

5. Yoh, pull through to the front.

6. Yoh and begin to pull through two loops...

7. ...so there are four loops on the hook. Yoh...

8. ...and pull through the remaining four loops.

9. Insert the hook in the next stitch, pushing the cluster away from you to the front of the work, yoh.

10. Work the next row in trebles.

SHELL PATTERNS

Groups of stitches worked into one stitch form shells, which can be used to make an attractive scalloped edging for a variety of items. You will need a number of stitches divisible by six with one stitch left over. On square or rectangular items, try to ensure that the dc of the shell edging falls at the corner. If the centre of a treble cluster falls at a corner, add two more trebles to it to provide enough ease to turn. Repeat the steps to the end of your work, then fasten off.

1. Make 1ch to lift the hook to the right height.

2. Miss two stitches, insert the hook in next stitch...

3. ...and work five trebles in stitch.

4. Miss 2 sts, work 1dc in the next stitch. Repeat to the end.

FABRICS USING SHELLS

Working a second row into a row of shells removes the scalloped look, and adding more rows produces an attractive all-over pattern for fabric. This can be done by working treble clusters that look like inverted shells, using smaller clusters at the beginning and end of each row. Start with the shell edging, worked into a chain that is a multiple of six stitches plus one.

1. Work 3ch, turn. Work an 'unfinished' treble into the first stitch...

2. ..and another into the next stitch.

3. Yoh, pull through all three loops on the hook (tr2tog completed).

4. Work 3ch, then work 1dc into the centre treble of the 5tr shell.

5. Work 3ch...

6. ...then work one 'unfinished' treble in each of the next five stitches.

7. Yoh and draw through all five stitches.

8. Repeat steps 4–7 to the end of the row.

Sugar and Spice

This simple top for a child is worked in shells, in ribbon yarn, but the same pattern can be made in lightweight baby aran. The back and front are identical. The main instructions are for Size 1, and those in brackets are for the larger Size 2. The little bag and hair scrunchie make the perfect accessories.

Top

The front and back are alike. Make 63 (73) ch.
Row 1: 1tr in 4th ch from hook, 1 tr in each st to end, 3ch, turn 61 (71) sts
Row 2: 2tr in same place, miss 4 sts *5tr in next st, rep from * to last 5 sts, miss 4 sts, 3tr in last st, 1ch, turn.
Row 3: 1htr, 2tr, *1htr, 1dc, 1htr, 2tr, rep from * to last 2 sts, 1htr 1dc, 3ch, turn
Rep Rows 2 and 3 five (7) times.

Armholes

Row 12: ss over 5 (10) sts to centre tr of 5tr shell, 3ch, work as for row 2 to last 5 (10) sts, 1ch, turn (51 sts).
Row 13: as row 3.
Rep rows 2 and 3 six times.
Work row 2 once, 3ch, turn.
Next row: 1tr in each st to end of second shell (12 sts). Fasten off. Rejoin yarn to first st in the last but one complete shell, 3ch, work 1tr in each of next 11 sts to take you to end. Fasten off.
Work another piece to match.

Making up

Join shoulders and side seams using dc on WS, or sew together, taking care not to pull stitches too tightly, so the lower edge border can be worked in one piece.

Border

Note for Size 1: there will be 122 stitches around the lower edge of your work, but 126 are needed for the border. Mark the central stitch on back and front, and a stitch at each side seam. To increase the stitch count, work twice into each marked stitch.

Note for Size 2: there will be 142 stitches around the lower edge of your work, but only 140 are needed for the border. Decrease one stitch at each side to lose the extra two stitches. Join yarn to side seam and work into foundation chain again.

Rnd 1: 3ch, 2tr, *3ch, work 1tr in each of next 7 sts without missing any sts, rep from * to last 4 sts, 3ch, 4tr, ss to beg of rnd.
Rnd 2: with RS facing ss to 3chsp, 5tr in same 3chsp, 3ch, ss in first of these 3ch to form a picot (p), 4tr in same 3chsp, *5tr 1p 4tr in next 3chsp, rep from * to end. Break off yarn.

To complete

Sew sequins on to the border and the first two rows of the front and back pieces.

You will need

300g ribbon yarn (350g for Size 2)

5.00mm hook

Elastic hair tidy, 5cm (2in) in diameter

Small sequins to trim

Tension: 5 sts and 4 rows measure 5cm (2in)

Size 1: to fit chest 62cm (24in); length from shoulder 32cm (12½in)

Size 2: to fit chest 72cm (28in); length from shoulder 37cm (13½in)

Bag

Make 20ch.

Row 1: 1dc in 3rd ch from hook, 1dc in each ch to end, 1ch, turn (19 sts).

Row 2: 1dc in each st to end, 1ch, turn.

Rep row 2 until work measures 17cm (6¾ in).

Drawstring row: make 4ch (including 1ch for turning), *miss 1 st, 1tr in next st, rep from * to end.

Final row: ss in sp, 3ch, 4tr in same sp, *miss 1sp, 5tr in next sp, rep from * to end. Fasten off.

Rejoin yarn to base of bag. Work drawstring row in foundation ch. Work final row.

To complete

Sew on sequins. With RS facing and using dc, join sides. Make two 38cm (15in) chain lengths. Beginning at one side, thread one length through drawstring holes. Knot the ends together securely. Beginning at the other side, repeat with the second length.

Hair Scrunchie

Make a slip knot and join yarn to hair tidy by working 1dc over elastic.

Rnd 1: 41dc over elastic. Join with ss (42 sts).

Rnd 2: 1ch, 1dc in same place, *2dc in next st. Rep from * to end. Join to turning ch with ss (84 sts).

Rnd 3: 1ch, 1dc in same place, 5ch, miss 3 sts, *1dc, 5ch, miss 3 sts, rep from * to end. Join to turning ch with ss (21 chsps).

Rnd 4: ss to next 5chsp, 1ch in same sp, 1htr 4tr 1htr 1dc in same sp, *1 dc 1htr 4tr 1htr 1dc in next chsp, rep from * to end, ss to beg of rnd.

Fasten off.

The finished Sugar and Spice Top, Hair Scrunchie and Bag.

51

TEXTURE

The names of textured stitches are not standardised, so take care. The same stitch may be known as a bobble, cluster, popcorn or puff stitch. Texture is created by putting groups of stitches in one place to give crocheted fabric an embossed look. Regular stitches should be worked between the textured stitches to help them to fit into the row and enhance the embossed look.

PUFF STITCH

This stitch is made by working several loops in one place, then drawing the yarn through all the loops. Like all bobble-type stitches, it is more effective when it is worked in rows of shorter stitches. To produce even tension, do not collect stitches in the narrower section of hook near the head; place them on to the stem. For a more pronounced effect, increase the number of loops in the stitch to nine or even eleven.

WORKING A PUFF STITCH

1. Yoh, insert the hook where you want the puff...

2. ...yoh and pull through, tilting the hook to make a large loop.

3. Repeat three times (seven loops on the hook), yoh...

4. ...and pull through all seven loops on the hook.

5. Work 1ch.

6. Push the puff stitch away from you. Insert the hook in the next stitch.

Tip
The second and subsequent rows of puff stitch will be easier to work if you fold the stitches of the puff stitch below and hold them between your thumb and forefinger before inserting the hook.

TRIAL PIECE

Start with 23ch.
Row 1: 1tr in 4th ch from hook, 1 tr in each st to end, 1ch, turn.
Row 2: 1dc, *1puff, 3dc, rep from * to last 3 sts, 1puff, 2dc, 3ch, turn.
Row 3: 1tr in each st to end, 1ch, turn.
Rep rows 2 and 3 to length required.

POPCORNS

Clusters can flatten with use, particularly when they are made from soft acrylic or wool yarn, but popcorns retain their texture even after pressing. This method brings the popcorn to the front; for one at the back, insert the hook from back to front. Some patterns add 1ch *after* the completion of each popcorn, but this may be confusing. If you remember to work into the back of the popcorn, where the loop was drawn through, on the next row, all should be well.

WORKING A POPCORN

1. Place five complete trebles into one stitch.

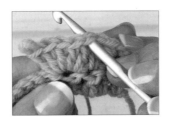

2. Remove hook. Insert, front to back, in first tr.

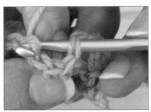

3. Collect the loose loop...

4. ...and pull it through to the front.

5. Work 1tr in the next stitch.

TRIAL PIECE
Begin with 23ch.
Row 1: 1tr in 4th ch from hook, 1tr in each st to end, 3ch, turn.
Row 2: 1dc, *1 popcorn (see right), 3dc, rep from * to last 3 sts, 1 popcorn, 2dc, 3ch, turn.
Row 3: 1tr in each st to end, 3ch, turn.
Rep rows 2 and 3 to length required.

BOUCLÉ STITCH

The trial piece shown below features the taller double treble in a row of dc. To achieve the tightest 'bobble', work with the wrong side facing. Ideally, alternate rows should be worked in either double crochet, half treble, or treble.

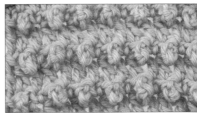

WORKING BOUCLÉ STITCH

1. Work 1dtr after a dc.

2. Insert the hook for the next dc pushing dtr away from you.

3. Complete the dc.

TRIAL PIECE
Start with 23ch.
Row 1: 1tr in 4th ch from hook, 1tr in each st to end, 1ch, turn.
Row 2: *1dtr, 1dc to end, 3ch, turn.
Row 3: 1tr in each st to end, 1ch, turn.
Rep rows 2 and 3 to length required.

Cuddly Cover

This smart and cosy pram cover would make the perfect gift for a special new baby. If you would prefer to make a cover for a crib or cot, it is easy to adjust the size by adding multiples of 8ch to create extra panels, and working more rows.

Cover

Using M, make 66ch.
Row 1: 1dc in 2nd ch from hook, 1dc in each ch to end (65 sts).
Row 2: 3ch *miss 3dc, 4tr 2ch 4tr in next st (1 shell made), miss 3dc, 1 puff in next st (see page 52), rep from * 6 times, miss 3dc, 1 shell in next st, miss 3dc, 1tr in last st.
Row 3: 3ch, 1 shell in 2ch space of shell, *work 1 puff around puff of row below (insert hook to right of, behind, and out to the front of puff to twist it and produce a cabled effect), 1 shell in shell, rep from * to last st, 1tr in last st, 3ch, turn.
Row 4: 1 shell in 2ch space of shell, *work 1 puff around puff of row below (insert hook from the back to the front of the work, to the right of and in front of puff, then return it to the back so the twist stays on RS of fabric), 1 shell in shell, rep from **to last st, 1tr in last st, turn.
Rep rows 3 and 4 a further 11 times and row 3 once, or to length required.
Note: the turnback starts here.
Row 27: As row 3.
Row 28: As row 4.
Rep rows 3 and 4 twice.

Edging (ribbon carrier row)

With WS facing, work along the turnback edge †† 1 shell in 2chsp of shell, 1dc in puff. Rep from †† to corner continuing to work down the longer side, 5ch *1tr in next row end, 2ch, rep from * to corner, 1tr 3ch 1tr in corner st # 2ch, 1tr in base of next shell on row 2, 2ch, 1tr in puff st on row 2, rep from # to next corner, 2ch, 1tr 3ch 1tr in corner st, rep from * to # once, omitting last 3ch 1tr of corner. Fasten off.

Shell edging

Note: the edging is worked in two sections to ensure that the shells look the same when the flap is turned down.
Connect M to 7th space from top.
Row 1 (RS facing): 1ch *miss 1 space, 9dtr in next space, miss 1 space, 1dc in next space, rep from * to corner, 13dtr in corner space, miss 1 space, 1dc in next space,** rep from * to ** once. Continue working shell edge but stop 7 spaces from top. Fasten off. Turn. With RS facing, work shell edging around rest of cover.
Last row: Using C, work 1 crab stitch in each st. Join with ss.
Trim as required to complete.

You will need

300g baby chunky or baby aran weight yarn in main colour (M)

25g same yarn in a contrasting colour (C)

6.00mm hook

2m (78in) ribbon for trim and small motifs for decoration.

Size: 51cm x 71cm (20 x 28 in) or 53cm (21in) with flap turned down

Tension: from the centre of one cable to the centre of the next cable measures 5cm (2in), worked on a 6.00mm hook

Tip

To work a puff stitch around one in the previous row, insert the hook so that it picks up the puff stitch and pulls it to the front or back as required. A similar principle is used to produce raised treble stitches – see page 56.

The finished Cuddly Cover
*This is worked in traditional baby white but given
a modern twist by the use of deep blue for the
edging and ribbon trim. There is no limit to the
number of possible colour variations – have fun
choosing your own.*

RAISED TREBLE

When raised trebles or raised long trebles are included in crocheted fabric, they add texture so it resembles knitted aran fabric. Aran effects can also be produced by adding surface chains, but I find it easier to use raised stitches worked at the same time as the crocheted fabric.

Raised stitches are made by inserting the hook to the right of a stitch and taking it across to emerge at the left. This pushes the stitch forward or backwards, depending on how the hook is inserted, making ridges and giving the work an 'embossed' look. The 'stem' on trebles makes this easy to do.

RAISED TREBLE FRONT (RTRF)

A raised treble front (RtrF) pulls the stitch forward.

1. Yoh, insert the hook from right to left around the stem of the stitch below.

2. Yoh, draw the hook from behind the stem (three loops on the hook).

3. Yoh, draw through two loops...

4. ...yoh and draw through the remaining two loops to complete the stitch.

RAISED TREBLE BACK (RTRB)

This is worked in a similar way to a RtrF. The hook is inserted from right to left around the stem of the treble, but from *behind* the fabric. This pushes the stem of the treble to the back.

1. Yoh and *working from the back*, insert the hook from right to left around the stem of the stitch below.

2. Take the hook out to the back, pushing the treble away from the work, yoh...

3. ...and pull through (three loops on the hook).

4. Yoh and pull through two loops, yoh as shown...

5. ...and complete the stitch.

RAISED TREBLE RIB (RTR RIB)

Fabric worked using alternate front and back raised trebles is very 'elastic' and ideal for a ribbed welt or collar. The more rows worked, the stronger the elasticated effect. The first row worked into the chain is not elastic, so all raised treble ribs should be worked *outwards* from the main body of the fabric.

To add crocheted rib to fabric, work directly around the stems of the stitches in the first row. For a welt, put the back and fronts together and start working the rib downwards. For the best results on a neckband, pick up and work the stitches around the front and shoulders, work a row of htr, then start the rib pattern. Try the following sample, choosing a hook a size smaller than for the fabric. Repeat for at least 10 rows.

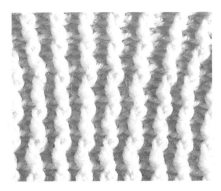

Detail ribbing from the Cosy Coat shown on page 60.

TRIAL PIECE

Make 20ch (18 sts).

Row 1: 1tr in 4th ch from hook, 1tr in each st to end, 2ch, turn.

Row 2: *1RtrF,1RtrB, rep from * to last st, Rtr around last st inserting hook in space in the relevant direction, 2ch, turn.

Repeat Row 2 to the length required.

A raised treble front being worked.

A raised treble back being worked.

Tip

Make sure all raised trebles are in a continuous line. On third and subsequent rows, or when there is an odd number of stitches, this will help you keep track of your place.

Look at the previous row to decide whether the next stitch was pushed back or pulled forward. If it was pushed back, begin the row with a RtrB. If it was pulled forward, start this row by working a RtrF.

CABLES

Most cable effects are worked using the longer raised trebles on a background of trebles or half trebles, rather than double crochet. A RdtrF is made in the same way as a RtrF – see page 56 – with one more wrap of the yarn.

Follow the steps below until you are happy with the technique for making cables, then increase your expertise by practising the addition of ghost stitches.

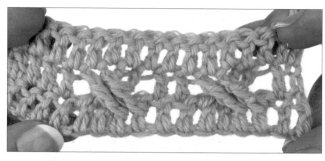

Cable sample worked without ghost stitches

1. Miss two stitches, yoh twice, insert the hook in the next stitch as shown...

2. ...and work RdtrF in the next stitch.

3. Yoh twice and insert the hook again...

4. ...to complete two RdtrF stitches.

5. Return to the first missed st, yoh twice, insert the hook...

6. ...and work a RdtrF in the stitch.

7. Yoh, insert the hook in the second missed stitch...

8. ...and work another RdtrF to complete two dtr cables (a four-stitch cable).

CABLES WITH GHOST STITCHES

When the crossed stitches that produce cabled effects are made, holes can appear at the side. One way to prevent this is by using 'ghost' stitches. These extra stitches are worked between the cable and the next treble to fill the gap without increasing or decreasing the overall number of stitches, and they are not counted. They can be introduced to any pattern with raised treble cabling – see Cosy Coat, page 60.

Cables worked with ghost stitches

WORKING GHOST STITCHES

1. Insert the hook and work a treble until two loops remain.

2. Miss 1st, work 1RdtrF around the next stitch until three loops remain.

3. Yoh and draw through all three loops.

4. Work 1RdtrF in next st and 1RdtrF in st below tr worked in step 1, then work 1RdtrF in the missed st until two loops remain.

5. Work 1tr in top of the second RdtrF worked...

6. ...until three loops remain on the hook...

7. ...to complete a 4dtr cable with ghost stitches.

EASY BUTTONS

Buttons can be made very easily by working trebles into a slip knot which will open to accommodate them. Gather the outside of the resulting circle and fill firmly with a small ball of the same yarn to make a washable and useful button. For a different effect, insert an old button, a bead, or even a coin.

1. Make a slip knot – see page 16 – 3ch, insert the hook in the knot...

2. ...and work eleven trebles into it...

3. Join into a circle with ss. Draw up the slip knot.

4. Wind off a tiny ball of the same yarn.

5. Fasten off the yarn leaving a long end. Thread this into a darning needle and weave the yarn through the outside edge of the circle.

6. Draw the edges together, inserting the tiny ball of yarn before you close the gap. Fasten off.

Cosy Coat

This aran-style coat looks much heavier than it is. It drapes beautifully to flatter the figure and give an air of elegance. The main instructions are for Size 1, and those in brackets are for the larger Size 2.

Special Abbreviation: Cable (worked over 4 sts)
Work a tr until there are two loops on the hook, miss 1 st, work 1RdtrF until there are three loops on the hook, yoh and draw through all three loops. Work 1RdtrF in the next st, 1RdtrF where the 'unfinished' tr was placed, 1 'unfinished' RdtrF in st missed (2 loops on hook), 1 unfinished tr in top of last st of 4st gr (3 loops on hook) yoh, draw through all 3 loops.

Back

Using 6.00mm hook work 74 (78) ch.
Row 1: 1htr in 4th ch from hook, 1htr in each ch to end, 2ch, turn (72 [76] sts).
Row 2 (RS): 3 (5) htr, *1RtrF, 1htr, 1RtrB, 1 Cable (see *Special Abbreviation*), 1RtrB, 1htr, rep from * 6 times, 1RtrF, 4 (6) htr, 2ch, turn.
Row 3: 3 (5) htr, 1RtrB, *1htr, 1RtrF, 4RtrF, 1RtrF, 1htr, 1RtrB, rep from * 6 times, 4 (6) htr, 2ch, turn.
Rows 2 and 3 form patt. Rep to length required. Place a marker 4 rows from top.

Left front

Using 6.00mm hook work 40 (42)ch
Row 1: 1htr in 4th ch from hook, 1htr in each ch to end, 2ch, turn (38[40]sts).
Row 2 (RS): 3 (5) htr, *1RtrF, 1htr, 1RtrB, 1 Cable (see Special Abbreviation), 1RtrB, 1htr, rep from * twice , 1RtrF, 6htr, 2ch turn.
Row 3: 5htr, 1RtrB, *1htr, 1RtrF, 4RtrB, 1RtrF, 1htr, 1RtrB, rep from * twice, 4(6) htr, 2ch, turn.
Rows 2 and 3 form patt. Rep them until length is the same as to the back marker.

Shape neck

Row 1: work in patt over first 31 sts, 2ch, turn.
Row 2: *1RtrF, 4RtrB, 1RtrF, 1htr, 1RtrB, 1htr, rep from * once, RtrF, 4RtrB, 1RtrF, 1htr, 1RtrB, 4htr, 2ch, turn.
Row 3: work in patt over first 27 sts, 2ch, turn.
Row 4 (keeping patt continuous): 1htr, 1RtrF, 1htr, 1RtrB, *1htr, 1RtrF, 4RtrB, 1RtrF, 1htr, 1RtrB, rep from * once, 4htr, 2ch, turn.
Row 5: work in patt over first 24 sts, 1htr, 1ch, turn.
Row 6: miss 1 st, work in patt to end. Fasten off.

You will need

1500g aran weight yarn, 75% acrylic/25% wool (1600g for Size 2)

5.00mm, 6.00mm and 7.00mm hooks

2–3 clasps (optional)

Size 1: to fit bust 81–87cm (32–34in)

Size 2: to fit bust 91–97cm (36–38in)

Back length: 105cm (41in)

Sleeve seam: 48cm (19in)

Tension: 6htr and 5 rows measure 5cm (2in)

Note: when you work this garment, it is better to count the rows than to measure them.

Tip

Fashion crochet, including aran style garments, should not use more yarn than similar knitted items. Knitted aran fabric is much heavier than stocking stitch fabric, and aran-style crochet can be heavier than other crochet fabrics.

The finished Cosy Coat

Right front

With 6.00mm hook work 40 (42)ch.
Row 1: 1htr in 4th ch from hook, 1htr in each ch to end, 2ch, turn (38[40]sts).
Row 2 (RS): work 5htr, *1RtrF, 1htr, 1RtrB, 1 Cable, 1RtrB, 1htr, rep from * twice, 1RtrF, 4(6) htr, 2ch, turn.
Row 3: work 3(5) htr, 1RtrB, *1htr, 1RtrF, 4RtrB, 1RtrF, 1htr, 1RtrB, rep from * twice, 6htr, 2ch, turn.
Rows 2 and 3 form patt. Rep them until length is the same as to back marker.

Shape neck

Row 1: ss over 7 sts, 1ch, work in patt over rem 30 sts, 2ch, turn.
Row 2: work in patt over 29 sts, 1ch, turn.
Row 3: miss 2 sts, work next 2 sts as the last 2 sts of the cable, patt to end, 2ch, turn.
Row 4: work in patt over 27 sts, 2ch, turn.
Row 5: work 1RtrB over next Rtr, patt to end, 2ch, turn.
Row 6: work in patt over 24 sts, 1htr. Fasten off.

Sleeve

Note: the sleeve starts with a shoulder insertion, then chain is added to both sides of the top – see page 38. Before you begin each sleeve, wind off and set aside about 1.3m (50in) of yarn for sleeve heading.

Make 2 alike.
Using the 6.00mm hook, make 14ch.
Row 1: 1htr in 4th ch from hook, 1htr in each ch to end, 2ch, turn (12 sts).
Row 2 (RS): 1RtrF, 1htr, 1RtrB, 1Cable, 1RtrB, 1htr, 1RtrF, 1htr, 2ch, turn.
Row 3: 1RtrB, 1htr, 1RtrF, 4RtrB, 1RtrF, 1htr, 1RtrB, 1htr, 2ch, turn.
Rows 2 and 3 form patt. Rep them 7 times or until the length, without stretching, is the same as to the unshaped last row of the front.

Sleeve heading

Make 32ch, leave last ch on a safety pin. With length of yarn set aside, work 30ch. Link this chain to the top of the turning ch on the last row of shoulder insertion using a ss. Fasten off. There are now two sleeve extensions. Return to loop in safety pin to continue sleeve.
Row 18: 1htr in 4th ch from hook, 29htr over chain extension, 1htr to reach patt section, 1RtrF, 1htr, 1RtrB, 1Cable, 1RtrB, 1htr, 1RtrF, 31htr, 2ch, turn (74 sts).
Rows 19–21: keeping central panel in patt and all other stitches in htr, work 3 rows.
Row 22: dec 1 st at each end of row (72sts).

Row 23: work as normal.
Rep these 2 rows 16 times (44 sts).
Work without dec until sleeve measures 35cm (16in) from chain extensions, ending with RS facing.
Next row (WS): 2ch, 13htr, 1RtrB, 8htr, 1RtrB, 14htr, 2ch, turn.
Dec row: (1RtrF, 1RtrB) 8 times, 1RtrF, 1RtrB around 2 sts, (1RtrF, 1RtrB) 9 times.
Work 2 rows Rtr rib. Change to 5.00mm hook and work 4 rows Rtr rib. Fasten off.

Inserting the sleeves

Do not join side or sleeve seams. Insert shoulder pieces between fronts and back of coat either by sewing or by working dc through both layers. Check that the back and the fronts match, and that both sides are the same.

Collar

Join in yarn. With 5.00mm hook and RS facing, work 2ch, 9htr across front, (1htr dec) 44 times to same point on opposite side, 10htr (64 sts), 2ch, turn.
Work 4 rows Rtr rib (see page 57).
Note: the row facing should be the wrong side as you look at the coat, but will be the right side of the turned-over collar.
Change to the 6.00mm hook. Work 2tr in same place as turning ch, *continue in Rtr rib to the sts that lie over the centre st of the shoulder insertion, inc 2 sts by working 1tr in top of the Rtr before the next st, 1Rtr, 1tr in top of Rtr after st just worked, rep from * once, work in Rtr rib to end, work 2 further tr in last st, 2ch, turn.
Work 3 rows Rtr rib.
Change to the 7.00mm hook and work 4 rows Rtr rib. Fasten off.

To complete

Join the tops of the sleeves to the fronts and back of coat either by sewing or by working dc through both layers. Place side markers 30cm (12in) from the hem on the fronts and back. With WS of coat facing, join the underarm sleeve seams either by sewing or by working dc through both pieces of work. Start at the cuff and work down the side seam to the markers. Fasten off. Add clasps to the front of the coat if desired.

LACE CROCHET

Lace is usually worked with a small hook and fine cotton thread, rather than the type of yarn that is favoured by knitters. Working with thread is a little different because it is not quite as 'user-friendly' as yarn made from wool, acrylic and soft spun cotton. These tips should help you to make a start.

CHOOSING YOUR HOOK

Cotton thread is defined by numbers: the lower the number, the thicker the thread. Thickness can range from a very fine No. 100 to the very thick No. 3. The most popular are No. 20 and No.10, which is sometimes known as bedspread weight. For household items in No. 20 cotton, try a 1.50mm hook, or a 1.75mm hook for No. 10. For fashion items in No. 20 cotton try a 2.00mm hook, or a 2.50mm hook for No. 10. The suggested hook sizes should be regarded as a starting point. You will need to experiment with your chosen thread before deciding whether you need to change your hook for a larger or smaller size.

WORKING WITH FINE COTTON

Thread does not have the elasticity of yarn so every tiny difference in the tension will be noticeable. If you are relaxed one day but more stressed the next, the look of your work may change, and unfortunately this is just a little more obvious with cotton! If you move your finger up or down the hook, the size of the stitches will vary and your work will look irregular and ugly. The best way to avoid this is to place a finger on the hook and use it as a 'stop'. If you always keep your 'stopping' finger in the same place, all the loops you work will be to the same tension and will end up in the same place.

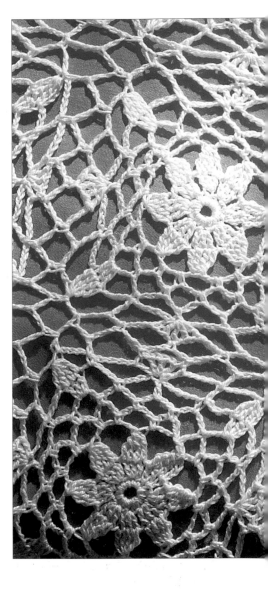

Lace crochet holding technique, using the finger as a 'stop'.

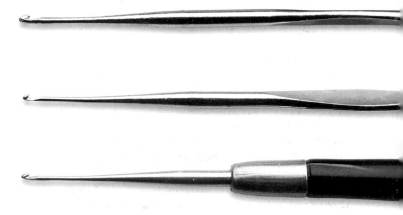

Hooks suitable for cotton

Cute Camisole

This little top is ideal for wearing under a suit jacket. Try it in lurex for evening or cotton for summer. It is worked using a method that avoids joins: the first half is worked sideways and fastened off, then the second half is worked in the opposite direction from the same foundation chain. This keeps the work very flat, with no ridges to rub the skin.

Main part

Make 72ch for the first half of the garment.
Row 1: 2tr in 4th ch from hook, *miss 1ch, 2tr in next ch, rep from * to last 2 sts, miss 1ch, 1tr in last ch, 3ch, turn (33 tr grs plus 2 end sts).
Row 2: *2tr in centre of tr gr, rep from * to end, 1tr in top of turning ch, 3ch, turn.
Rep row 2 until work measures 43cm (17in), or half the bust size required for the finished garment plus 2.5cm (1in). Check that the number of rows is divisible by four plus one, which will make it easier to work the trim at the lower edge. Fasten off.

Second half

Return to the foundation chain and work into the other side.
Join yarn to end st, 3ch, *miss 1ch, 2tr in base of original 2tr on foundation ch, rep from * to last 2 sts, miss 1ch, 1tr in last st, 3ch, turn.
Work until second half is the same length as the first. Do not break off yarn; the front edging is worked continuously. No turning chain are required.

Front and top edging

*5tr in next gr, ss in next gr, rep from * to last gr, 9tr in last gr, ss in next row end, # 5tr in next row end, ss in next row end, rep from # around top to corner. Fasten off.

Lower edging

With RS (the side from which the last border was worked) facing, join yarn to corner st.
Row 1: 1ch, *1dc in next row end, miss 1 row end, (1dtr 3ch 1dtr) in next row end, miss 1 row end, rep from * to end, 1dc in last row end, 1dc in last st, 3ch, turn.
Row 2: 1tr in dc, *(3dtr 1ch 3dtr) in 3chsp, 1tr in dc, rep from * to end, 1tr in last st, ss into base of front edge, 1ch, turn.
Row 3: 1tr in tr, *(4dtr 1picot 3dtr) in 3ch sp, 1htr in dc, rep from * to end, 1tr in last st. Fasten off.

Shoulder straps

(Make two alike). Work a length of chain that is a multiple of 4 sts plus 2. Thread is less stretchy than yarn but the straps may still stretch: take care not to make them too long.
Row 1: 2tr into 4th ch from hook, *miss 1ch, 2tr in next ch, rep from * to last 2 sts, 1tr in last st, 1ch to turn.
Row 2: *5tr in centre of 2tr gr, 1dc in next 2tr gr, rep from * to end. Fasten off. Make another strap the same.

To complete

Attach the straps to the top, placing the straight edge towards the neck.

You will need

150g No. 10 cotton

2.00mm hook

Size: to fit bust 81cm (32 in) or size required

Tension: 15sts and 9 rows measure 5cm (2in) worked over pattern

Note: the ease allowance for this garment is only 5cm (2in).

The finished Cute Camisole top

FILET CROCHET

Filet is a simple squared network of blocks and spaces in chain and trebles. It is good for household textiles, especially when used flat on upholstery or wooden surfaces so the pattern shows clearly. It is also good for fashion items, particularly edgings. As with all crochet, hook size is determined by yarn thickness.

Filet is usually worked in mercerised cotton, but smooth yarn in mixed fibres can be used. Textured yarns can detract from its crispness and reduce the impact of a design. Work a trial piece to check the tension and the effect of the yarn.

INCREASING WITH A BLOCK OR SPACE

Filet must be shaped at each end of a row to keep work symmetrical. Because it is worked in squares, increases and decreases produce a series of steps. A curved edge can only be achieved by adding an edging to the completed item. Increasing at the beginning of a row of filet is easy: just add extra chains at the end of the row before. If the last stitch of the row before is a treble, add 7ch to make a space.

1. Work 7ch at the end of the row before turning.

2. Turn and insert the hook in the 4th ch along.

3. Work the increase block into the chain.

INCREASING AT THE END OF A ROW

To add a block, work a double treble in the same place as the last treble of the previous row. Work a *second* double treble in the lower segment of the first double treble and a third in the lower segment of the second. Finish with a treble in the lower segment of the last double treble. The lower segments of the double trebles will bend and effectively become the base chain of the new block.

Note: to increase by a space at the end of a row, work 2ch, 1 trtr in the same place as the last treble of the block.

The completed increase.

1. Work 1dtr in the same place as the last treble of the row.

2. Work a second dtr into the lower segment of the first dtr...

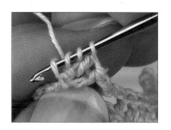

3. ...then a third dtr in the lower segment of the second dtr.

4. Work a treble in the lower segment of the last double treble.

INCREASING WITH A SPACE

Adding a space at the end of a row of filet crochet is easy if you use a long stitch, in this case the quadruple treble, in the same place as the last stitch.

1. Work 1 tr in the last stitch of the row, 2ch...

2. ...yoh four times...

3. ...and work a quadtr...

4. ...to produce a very neat space increase.

DECREASING IN FILET

Decreasing in filet is easy. At the beginning of a row, slip stitch over the top of one square, then carry on as in steps 1–3. At the end of the row, simply stop working one square from the end – see step 4 – then turn to start the next row.

1. Slip stitch over the top of one whole square.

2. Work chains for the next stitch...

3. ...and work trebles into the space.

4. Stop working a square before the end of the row.

MAKING YOUR OWN FILET PATTERNS

Most people prefer to work from a pattern when learning a new technique, but once you have learned the technique, the next step is to make your own designs. Filet crochet uses mathematics, so there is a simple formula for calculating how many chains you should make before working the first row.

   Use the formula below to calculate the number of foundation chains required for a piece of filet crochet. The example given is for a chart with six squares.

Formula	Chart with 6 squares starting with a block	Chart with 6 squares starting with a space
Multiply the number of squares by 3	18	18
Add 1ch	1	1
Add 2ch if starting with a block	2	2
Add a further 2ch if starting with a space	0	2
Total number of chains needed	21	23

Filet Dove

Filet crochet is ideal for working small pictures. This simple design would make a really special greetings card, or even a pocket to embellish a plain top.

Work 102ch
Row 1: 1tr in 4th ch from hook, 1tr in each ch to end, 3ch, turn (100sts).
Row 2: 6tr, *2ch, 4tr, (counts as 1sp and 1blk), rep from * to last 3 sts, 3tr, 3ch, turn.
Row 3: 1blk, *3sps, 1blk, rep from * to end, 3ch, turn.
Row 4: 2blks, 29sps, 2blks, 3ch, turn.
Row 5: 1blk, 1sp, 1blk, 27sps, 1blk, 1sp, 1blk, 3ch, turn.
Row 6: 2blks, 13sps, 4blks, 12sps, 2blks.
Follow the chart below to complete the picture. Fasten off.

Tip

Any cross stitch pattern can be used to produce filet crochet. Note that the finished design will be slightly wider and shorter, but you can counteract this effect by working the filet using double treble stitches.

You will need

20g No. 10 crochet cotton

1.75mm hook

Frame or mount 23 x 16.5cm (9 x 6½in)

Tension: 4 spaces in width and 5 spaces in height measure 2.5cm (1in)

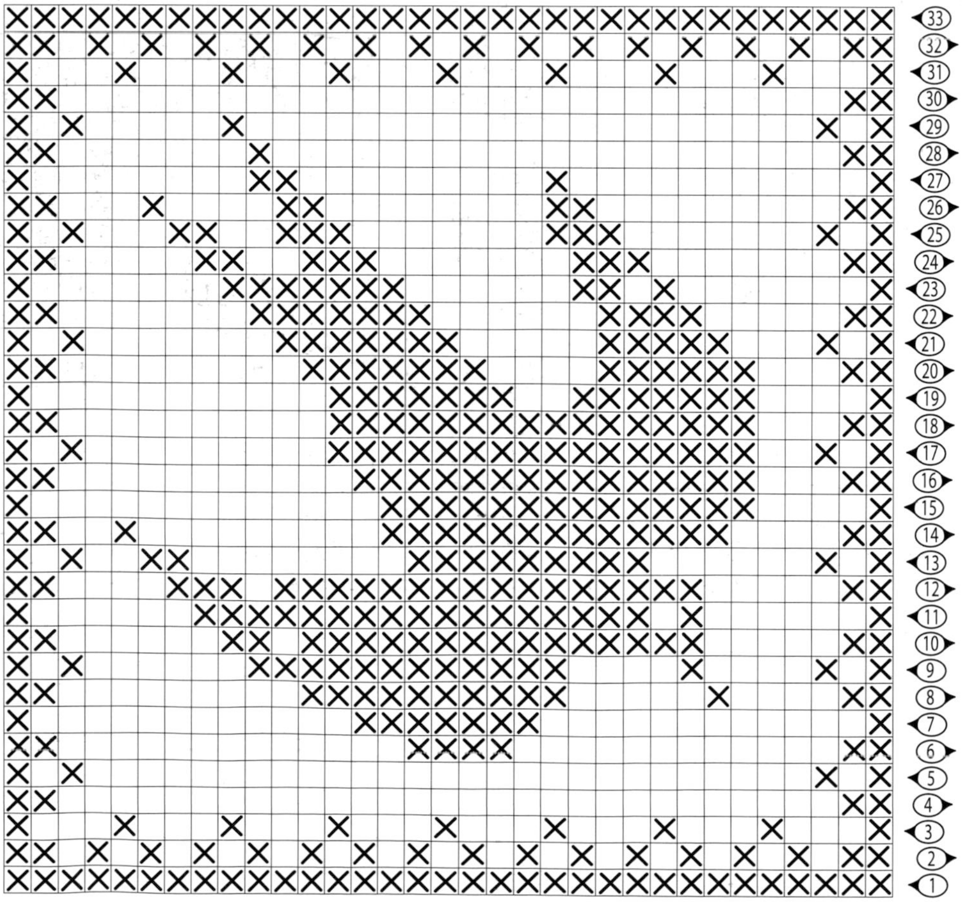

The chart for the Filet Dove

Key:

block = 3tr

space = 2ch 1tr

Each square with a cross represents a block of three trebles; each unmarked square a space made from 2ch, 1tr. When a block lies next to a space it looks as though it is made up of four trebles.

The arrows on the side of the numbered rows mark the direction in which you should be working: odd rows are worked from right to left and even rows are worked from left to right.

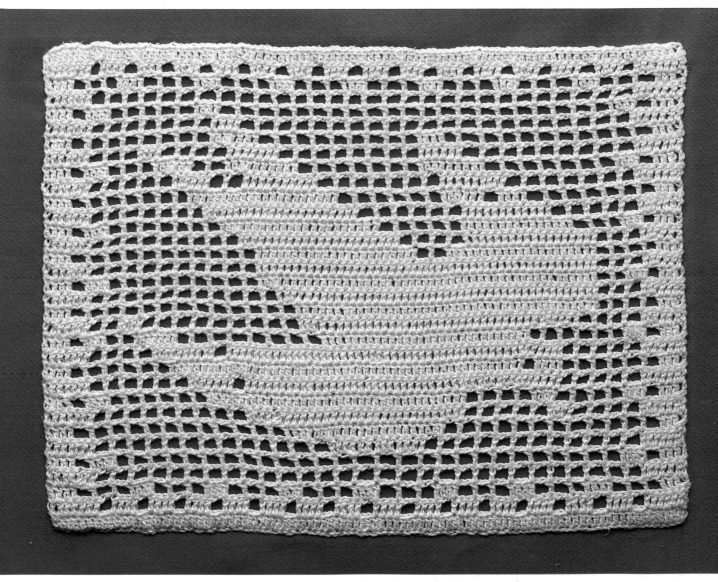

The finished Filet Dove

You can mount your finished filet crochet pictures in a picture frame for display. Pull your work from bottom to top to elongate the stitches and square individual blocks. Pin it out on contrasting backing fabric and oversew neatly to the fabric using finer thread in a matching shade. Place the fabric around the inner mount of a picture frame, making sure it is central to the frame. Trim away any excess so it fits exactly.

WORKING MOTIFS

The most common shape is the 'granny square' (see opposite) which is often worked in left-over yarn and made into blankets. Most geometric shapes are worked in rounds from the centre outwards: the way the increases are made determines whether a circle, hexagon, octagon, square or triangle is produced. If increases are made in the same three places on each round the result is a triangle, while if they are placed at the same six points, the result is a hexagon.

MAKING PERFECT CIRCLES

Circles should lie flat without frilling or cupping. The top of the stitches dictates the size of the circle because this cannot be changed as easily as the base. Stagger the increases on each round: if you place them on top of one another, you will produce little peaks with straight sections between. Complete each round by joining with a slip stitch, then work chains to represent the first stitch of the next round. These tips might help you to avoid disappointment:

Frilly edges
If this happens, there are too many stitches. Try one of the following:
a) work fewer increases per round.
b) check that you have not increased too many times.
c) use longer stitches to increase the diameter of the round.

Distorted centre
If the centre buckles when you change to a lacy pattern, check that you are not:
a) working the chains too tightly (buckling)
b) working the chains too loosely (frilling)
and if necessary, change your hook.

Bowl shape
If you produce a circle that is too tight around the edge, check that:
a) your stitches are not too tall
b) you are making sufficient increases on each round
c) the stitches are not too tight.

Tip
If you are not working to a pattern, turn your work on every round. This stops the joining seam looking as if it is on a diagonal. If you do not work each round separately, the result will be a spiral, and you will be unable to complete your work without producing an ugly step.

PLANNING MOTIFS				
Process	double crochet	half treble	treble	double treble
Start with:	4ch	4ch	4ch	5ch
Join with:	1ss	1ss	1ss	1ss
Make:	1ch	2ch	3ch	4ch
Place stitches in the centre of ring:	5dc	7htr	11tr	23dtr
Join with:	1ss	1ss	1ss	1ss
Make:	1ch	2ch	3ch	4ch
Turn motif, work 1 st in same place as start of turning chain:	2dc in each st	2htr in each st	2tr in each st	2dtr in each st
This gives an increase per round of:	6dc	8htr	12tr	24dtr
Continue to increase on each round by:	6dc	8htr	12tr	24dtr
The increases even after 50 rounds should be the same as for round 2, which is:	6dc	8htr	12tr	24dtr

OTHER SHAPES

Motifs begin as a circle and take shape as you work. For a square, the number of increases must be divisible by four.

Granny square

These are traditionally made in three colours.

Make 4ch with colour 1. Join into ring with ss.
Rnd 1: 3ch, 2tr into ring, *1ch, 3tr, rep from * twice, 1ch. Join to top of 3ch at beg of row with ss. Fasten off.
Rnd 2: Join in colour 2 to any 1ch sp, 3ch, 2tr 1ch 3tr in same sp, *3tr 1ch 3tr in next sp, rep from * twice. Join to top of turning ch with ss. Fasten off.
Rnd 3: Join in colour 3 to any corner sp, 3ch, 2tr 1ch 3tr in same sp, * 3tr in next sp, 3tr 1ch 3tr in corner sp, rep from * twice, 3tr in remaining side sp. Join to top of turning ch with ss. Fasten off.

Pin motif

This tiny motif is also a useful 'filler' for a space left when motifs are joined.

Make 6ch. Join into ring with ss.
Rnd 1: 1ch, 13dc in centre of ring, ss to top of ch.
Rnd 2: 3ch, *miss 1 st, 1htr in next st, 1ch, rep from * 5 times. Join to 2nd of 3ch at beg of row with ss.
Rnd 3: *1dc 1htr 2tr 1htr 1dc in next sp, rep from * to end. Join to last htr with ss. Fasten off.

Hexagon

For a hexagon, divide the number of increases per round by six and work them in six places only. In dc that means working an extra stitch for each stitch.

Make 4ch. Join into ring with ss.
Rnd 1: 1ch, 5dc in centre of ring. Join with ss.
Rnd 2: 3ch, 2tr in same place, *1ch, 3tr in next st, rep from * to end, 1ch, ss to top of turning ch.
Rnd 3: 3ch, tr2tog, *3ch, 1dc in 1chsp, 3ch, tr3tog, rep from * 4 times, 3ch, 1dc in 1chsp, 3ch, ss to beg of rnd.
Rnd 4: 5ch, *1tr in dc, 3ch, 1tr in top of cl, 3ch, rep from * 4 times, 1tr in dc, 3ch, ss to beg of rnd.
Rnd 5: 4ch, 1tr 1ch 1tr in same place, * 3ch, 1dc in next tr, 3ch, 1tr 1ch 1tr 1ch 1tr all in next tr, 3ch, rep from * 4 times, 3ch, 1dc in next tr, 3ch, ss to 3rd of 4ch at beg of rnd. Fasten off.

Petalled square

Make 8ch. Join into ring with ss.
Rnd 1: 1ch, 15dc into centre of ring. Join with ss.
Rnd 2: 4ch, miss 1 st, *1tr 3ch 1tr in next st, 1tr, miss 1 st, rep from * twice, 1tr 3ch 1tr in next st. Join to 3rd of 4ch at beg of rnd with ss.
Rnd 3: 1ch, *4tr 1ch 4tr in 3chsp, miss 1tr after the 3chsp, 1dc in next tr, rep from * to end omitting last dc, ss to top of turning ch.
Rnd 4: 5ch, 1quadtr 3ch 1quadtr 2ch 1dtr all in same place, *(1dtr 3ch 1trtr 3ch 1trtr 3ch 1dtr) all in 1chsp, (1dtr 2ch 1quadtr 3ch 1quadtr 2ch 1dtr) all in next dc, rep from * twice, (1dtr 3ch 1trtr 3ch 1trtr 3ch 1dtr) all in 1chsp. Join to 3rd of 5ch at beg of rnd with ss.
Rnd 5: *(1dc 1htr 1tr) in 2ch sp, (3tr 2ch 3tr) in 3ch sp, (1tr 1htr 1dc) in 2ch sp, (1dc 1htr 3tr) in next 3chsp, (4dtr 3ch 4dtr) in next 3chsp, (3tr 1htr 1dc) in next 3chsp, rep from * 3 times. Join with ss. Fasten off.

Picot circle

Make 5ch. Join into ring with ss.
Rnd 1: 7ch, ss in 4th ch from hook, (1 picot made). 1ch, *1tr, 1ch, 1p, 1ch, rep from * 6 times. Join to 3rd of 7ch at beg of rnd with ss.
Rnd 2: 9ch, *1dtr in top of tr, 5ch, rep from * 6 times. Join to 4th of 9ch at beg of rnd with ss.
Rnd 3: *ss to next sp, 1dc (1p, 2dc) 3 times, rep from * 7 times. Join to beg of rnd with ss. Fasten off.

Twelve petal flower

Special Abbreviation: quintr = quintuple treble. Wrap yarn around the stem of the hook five times before inserting the hook in the stitch. Take off the loops two at a time as for quadruple treble – see page 35.

Make 8ch. Join into ring with ss.
Rnd 1: 3ch, 23tr in centre of ring. Join to top of turning ch with ss.
Rnd 2: 5ch, *miss 1 st, 1tr in next st, 2ch, rep from * 10 times. Join to 3rd of 5ch with ss.
Rnd 3: ss in next sp, 7ch, 1quintr 5ch 2quintr in same place, *2quintr 5ch 2quintr in next sp, rep from * 10 times. Join with ss.
Rnd 4: ss to next chsp, 3ch, 11tr in same place, * 12tr in next sp, rep from * to end, ss to top of turning ch. Fasten off.

Kite

When this motif is joined, oval spaces are formed between the points. Interesting fillings can be used in these spaces.

Make 6ch. Join into ring with ss.
Rnd 1: 3ch, 1tr into centre of ring, *1ch, 2tr into centre of ring, rep from * 6 times, 1ch, ss to top of turning ch.
Rnd 2: ss to next chsp, 3ch, 1tr in same sp, *1ch, 2tr 2ch 2tr in next ch sp, 1ch, 2tr in next sp, rep from * twice, 1ch, 2tr 2ch 2tr in next ch sp, 1ch, ss to top of turning ch.
Rnd 3: ss to next chsp, 3ch, 1tr in same sp, *1ch, 3tr 2ch 3tr in next ch sp, 1ch, 2tr in next sp twice, rep from * twice, 1ch, 3tr 2ch 3tr in next ch sp, 1ch, ss to top of turning ch.
Rnd 4: ss to next chsp, 3ch, 1tr in same sp, * 4tr 3ch 4tr in next ch sp, 2tr in next sp 3 times, rep from * twice, 4tr 3ch 4tr in next ch sp, ss to top of turning ch.
Rnd 5: 1ch, *1dc in each tr to next 3chsp, 1dc 1htr 1tr 1dtr 1trtr 1dtr 1tr 1htr 1dc in 3chsp, rep from * 3 times, 1dc in each tr to beg of rnd, ss to beg of rnd. Fasten off.

Open square

Make 6ch. Join into ring with ss.
Rnd 1: 5ch, 3trtr in centre of ring, *3ch, 4trtr in centre of ring, rep from * 6 times, 3ch, ss to top of turning ch.
Rnd 2: ss to next chsp, 5ch, 3trtr in same sp, 3ch, 4trtr, *5ch, 1dc in chsp, 5ch, 4trtr 3ch 4trtr in next chsp, rep from * twice, 5ch, 1dc in chsp, 5ch, ss to the top of turning ch.
Rnd 3: ss to next chsp, 5ch, 3trtr in same sp, 3ch, 4trtr, *5ch, 1dc in chsp twice, 5ch, 4trtr 3ch 4trtr in next chsp, rep from * twice, 5ch, 1dc in chsp twice, 5ch, ss to top of turning ch.
Rnd 4: ss to next chsp, 5ch, 3trtr in same sp, 3ch, 4trtr, *5ch, 1dc in chsp 3 times, 5ch, 4trtr 3ch 4trtr in next chsp, rep from * twice, 5ch, 1dc in chsp 3 times, 5ch, ss to top of turning ch.
Rnd 5: ss to next chsp, 5ch, 3trtr in same sp, 3ch, 4trtr, *5ch, 1dc in chsp 4 times, 5ch, 4trtr 3ch 4trtr in next chsp, rep from * twice, 5ch, 1dc in chsp 4 times, 5ch, ss to top of turning ch.
Rnd 6: ss to next chsp, *5ch, 1dc in same sp, 5ch, 1dc in chsp 6 times, rep from *3 times, ss to beg of rnd.
Rnd 7: ss to next chsp, 1ch, 6dc in same sp, *7dc in next chsp, rep from * to end, ss to beg of rnd. Fasten off.

JOINING CIRCULAR MOTIFS

A small circular motif can be joined to a similar motif as the last row is worked. Circles can be attached to each other in rows and columns, or in the indentations made by rows of circles.

1. Make a small motif.

2. Make another motif to match leaving the last two repeats, *2ch.

3. Insert the hook under the corresponding loop of the previously worked motif.

4. Yoh and draw through (two loops on the hook).

5. Yoh and complete as 1dc...

6. ...work 2ch...

7. ...and insert the hook in the next chsp of motif.

8. Rep from * in step 2 to form the second link...

9. ...and produce the lacy look join.

Four motifs joined

ADDING A FILLER

If you want to place circular motifs in columns or rows, you will usually need to add a filler. The simplest way to do this is shown here.

1. Make a 6ch ring and fill with dc equal to the number of joins you want to make. Join with ss.

2. Make a chain that reaches the motif when it is slightly stretched. Join to the motif with a ss.

3. Make the same number of chain and return to the ring. Join it to the next dc with a ss.

4. Repeat these steps until you have worked all the link chains: the number of chains needed in each space depends on the size of the space.

JOINING SQUARES

Motifs with straight edges can be joined using dc on the wrong side. This gives a very neat join with movement, and works well if there is a right and a wrong side to the article – see example A.

Motifs joined with crab stitch produce a design line on the right side – see examples B and C.

You can also join motifs by oversewing using a flat stitch and a needle with a large eye – see example D.

A. Working dc on the wrong side.

B. Working crab stitch on the right side.

C. Contrasting crab stitch joins.

D. Joins made by oversewing.

Boudoir Pillow

The front of this little cushion is made from nine motifs, each linked to the next. If you prefer to make a single piece rather than motifs, the reverse of the cushion begins in the same way as a single motif but continues to form a large square.

Motif 1

Make 6ch. Join into ring with ss.
Rnd 1: 1ch, 15dc in centre of ring. Join to beg of rnd with ss.
Rnd 2: 3ch, 2tr in same place, 1ch, miss 1 st, *3tr in next st, 1ch, miss 1 st, rep from * 6 times. Join with ss.
Rnd 3: 4ch, dtr3tog over next 3 sts, *6ch, dtr4tog over next 4 sts, rep from * 6 times, 6ch. Join to top of 3 turning ch with ss.
Rnd 4: *4ch, 1dc in next 5chsp, 4ch 1dc in same chsp, rep from * 6 times, 4ch, 1dc in next 5chsp, 4ch, ss to beg of rnd.
Rnd 5: ss into 4chsp, *5ch, 1dc in next chsp, rep from * to last loop, 3ch, 1tr in beg of rnd.
Rnd 6: 3ch, 2tr in same sp, *5ch, 1dc in next 5chsp, 5ch, 1tr in next 5chsp, 5ch, 1dc in next 5chsp, 5ch, 3tr in next 5ch sp, rep from * 3 times omitting last 3tr. Join to top of 3 turning ch with ss.
Rnd 7: 4ch, dtr3tog over next 3 sts, *5ch, 1dtr in dc, 5ch, 1tr1ch 4 times in next tr to form a fan, 1tr in same place, 5ch, 1dtr in dc, 5ch, dtr4tog over next 4 sts, rep from * to end but omitting the last dtr4tog. Join to top of first cl with ss. Fasten off.

Motif 2

Work as Motif 1 but do not fasten off.

Linking motifs

Begin with Motif 2 (completed but not fastened off). 3ch, 1dc in first chsp on Motif 1, 3ch, 1dc in dtr on Motif 2, 3ch, 1dc in next chsp on Motif 1, 3ch, 1dc in first tr of gr on Motif 2, 3ch, 1dc in next chsp, 3ch, 1dc in last tr of gr on Motif 2, 3ch, 1dc in dtr on Motif 2, 3ch, 1dc in next chsp, 3ch, 1dc in cl. Fasten off.

Motif 3

Make as for Motif 2, linking motifs as above. Make two more strips of three motifs.

Joining the strips

Place two strips together, WS facing. Join thread to cl on front strip (S1).
*3ch, 1dc in 5chsp on back strip (S2), 3ch, 1dc in dtr of S1, 3ch, 1dc in 5chsp on S2, 3ch, 1dc in first chsp of fan on S1, 3ch, 1dc in central tr of fan on S2, 3ch, 1dc in last chsp of fan on S1, 3ch, 1dc in 5chsp on S2, 3ch, 1dc in dtr on S1, 3ch, 1dc in 5chsp on S2, 2ch 1tr in cl on S1, 3ch 1dc in sp by cl created by join of motifs on S2, 3ch, 1dtr in centre sp of join on S1, 3ch, 1dc in 2nd chsp created by join on S2, 3ch, 1dc in cl, rep from * twice. Fasten off.
Repeat these instructions to join remaining strip.

You will need

75g No. 10 cotton

1.75mm hook

25cm (10in) square cushion pad

Cover for pad

Size: 25 x 25cm (10 x 10in), before edging is worked

Tension: 1 motif measures 7.5 x 7.5cm (3 x 3in)

The front of the finished Boudoir Pillow.

Border

Rnd 1: join thread to centre tr of middle fan on one edge *3ch, 1tr in last tr of fan, (2ch 1dtr) 3 times in next dtr, 4ch, trtr3tog (place 1trtr in next cl, 1trtr in centre of join of strips, 1trtr in next cl), 4ch, work (1dtr 2ch) 3 times in next dtr, 1tr in first tr of fan, 3ch, ss in central tr of fan, † 3ch, 1tr in last tr of fan, (2ch 1dtr) 3 times in next dtr, (2ch 1dtr) 3 times in cl, (2ch 1dtr) 3 times in next dtr, 2ch, 1dtr in first tr of fan, 3ch, ss in central tr †† rep from * to † once and from * to †† once, ††† rep from * to ††† twice. Work from * to † once. to beg of round with d with ss.

Rnd 2: 3ch *(1tr 2ch) twice in next tr, 1tr 2ch 1tr in centre dtr of 3dtr gr, work 1trtr 2ch 1dtr 2ch 1dtr 2ch 1trtr all into central point of trtr cl, (1tr 2ch) twice in central dtr, 1ch, 1tr 2ch 1tr in next tr, 1ch, 1tr in ss 1ch †, (1tr 2ch) twice in next tr, (2ch 1tr) twice in central dtr, (2ch 1tr) twice in first dtr of corner gr, (2ch 1dtr) twice in central dtr of corner gr, (2ch 1tr) twice in last dtr of corner gr, (2ch 1tr) twice in next tr, 1ch, 1tr in ss, 1ch †† rep from * to † once, rep from * to †† once ††† rep from * to ††† twice, work from * to † once. Join to beg of rnd with ss. Fasten off.

Back

Rnds 1-5: work as motif on front.

Rnd 6: 3ch, 2tr in same place *(5ch 1dc in next chsp) 3 times, 5ch 3tr in next chsp, rep from * twice, (5ch, 1dc in next chsp) 3 times, 5ch. Join to top of turning ch with ss.

Rnd 7: ss to central tr of gr, 3ch, 2tr in same place, *(5ch 1dc in next 5chsp) 4 times, 5ch, 3tr in central tr of gr, rep from * twice, (5ch 1dc in next 5chsp) 4 times, 5ch. Join to top of turning ch with ss.

Rnd 8: ss to central tr of gr, 3ch, 2tr in same place *(5ch 1dc in next chsp) twice, 5ch, 3tr in next chsp, (5ch 1dc in next chsp) twice, 5ch, 3tr in central tr of gr, rep from * 3 times but omitting last 3tr. Join to top of turning ch with ss.

Rnd 9: as rnd 7 but rep instructions in brackets 6 times.

Rnd 10: as rnd 7 but rep instructions in brackets 7 times.

Rnds 11–13: as rnd 7 inc the number of times instructions in brackets are worked by one on each rnd.

Rnd 14: as rnd 8 but rep instructions in brackets 5 times.

Rnd 15–19: as rnd 7 inc the number of times the instructions in brackets are worked by one on each round from 12 to 16.

Rnd 20: as rnd 8 but rep instructions in brackets 8 times.

Rnds 21–25: as rnd 7 inc the number of times the instructions in brackets are worked by one on each round from 18 to 22.

Making up

With WS facing and using dc, join front and back on three sides. Continue along fourth side of the cushion but work dc along the edge of the back piece only. At the end of the fourth side turn so RS is facing. Work dc along the front piece to match the back. Do not turn. Work crab stitch along the unjoined front edge and around the joined three sides. Join with ss Insert a cushion pad and join back and front just below the round of crab stitch. Fasten off.

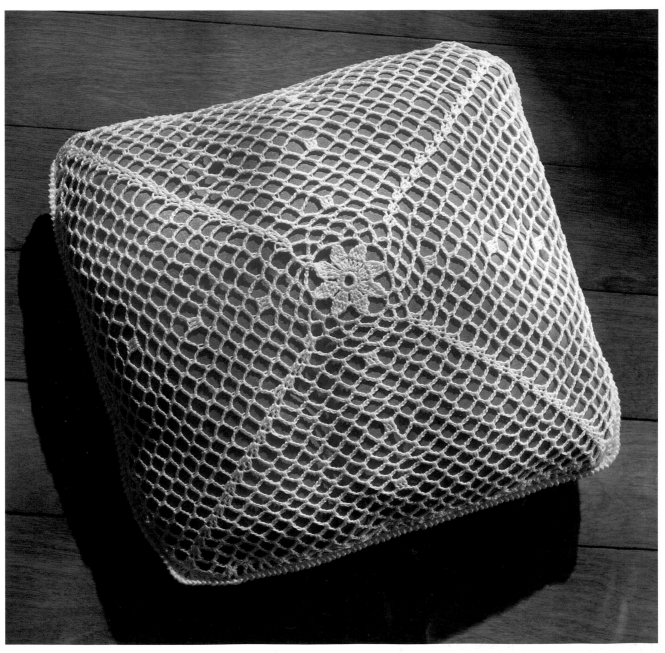

The back of the finished Boudoir Pillow.

Index